E N

It is both an honor and a privilege to write an endorsement for my beloved friend and heart sister Angela Greenig's incredible book. Angela is one of the most powerful seer warriors for our Lord Jesus Christ whom I have ever met. She is called like very few others to not only pierce the darkness, but to expose a multitude of the strategies of the enemy in the spirit realm. Believe me, dear reader, this incredible woman has not only laid her entire life down for the love of her profound insight into the spirit realm, but her accuracy as a seer and her powerful deliverance ministries are very unique on earth today.

I believe with all my heart that the keys to freedom and wisdom that exist in these pages will not only set you free, but infuse you with a divine passion to *go out* onto the highways and byways and set captives free. This is Angela's passion. This is an incredible woman walking in the spirit of power and might who lives every word that she writes and preaches. I believe that these pages hold the truth that so very many of us have been yearning and hungering for. She is not only one of the most powerful warriors I know, she is also my treasured, beloved friend who has warred on my behalf with power, faithfulness, and intense love. I love you so much, my beloved Angela. May thousands upon thousands come to freedom through reading these pages that you have scribed.

WENDY ALEC
Founder, GOD TV

Power and Authority Over Darkness, written by Angela Greenig, is a must-read. This book is a wake-up call for millions of Christians around the world. In this book Angela explains that "This is war," and we need each other like never before. United we stand, divided we fall. There is a new sound from Heaven in this book. You will be activated to carry out this new sound from Heaven. An awaking has begun! You are part of this new awakening. In a very clear and practical way, this book exposes darkness and satan's strategy to invade this generation. This book is a tool to overcome evil and to pierce the darkness. You will learn how to put your faith into action and how to remain in God's presence, even through your storms.

MATTHEUS VAN DER STEEN
Senior Pastor, House of Heroes, Netherlands
www.vandersteenministries.org

Angela's book, *Power and Authority Over Darkness,* is a powerful handbook and practical guide to spiritual warfare. The enemy is throwing everything he has at us right now because there is a generation rising up to take the Kingdom by storm. Angela's insight and anointing opens fresh new revelation on who we are, who God is, and who our enemy really is. Get ready to go to an entirely new level in the spirit!

DOUG ADDISON
Prophetic author of *Daily Prophetic Words*
and Spirit Connection, webcast and blog
www.DougAddison.com

We have the privilege of knowing Angela on a personal basis. News that she has written another book is always exciting! This book upholds relevance and an importance to this current age in which we are living. Angela has years of experience when it comes to equipping the church in the ministry of deliverance and strategy. Her knowledge comes partnered with wisdom and revelation. This book is not just a call to wake up, it is a training manual that qualifies and gives insight to forming strategies against the enemy.

It is time to take out the Goliaths and to walk out our birthrights as sons and daughters of our heavenly Father.

Peter and Anna Fagerhov

Senior Pastors, Nordanstigs Kristna Center, Sweden

www.NKC.be

In these turbulent times, it seems that everyone is discussing spiritual warfare in their sermons, books, and conferences. The problem is, spiritual warfare is a subject that many are teaching based on their ideas and thoughts. Angela Greenig teaches from her experience! She is a mighty woman of God who has stepped into her authority and has truly taken her place on the frontlines of ministry. I'm so thankful that she decided to share her insight, experience, and revelation with the body of Christ so we can be equipped and empowered for the battle! This isn't just a book for entertainment—this is a manual designed to open your eyes to the fullness of the victory that Jesus has given us, to which the gates of hell cannot prevail! Prepare to get *re-armed* and become *dangerous* to the kingdom of darkness!

Brad and Kayla Carter

Pastors, Kingdom Builders Ministries

North Carolina, USA

www.KingdomBuildersNC.org

Angela has rescued many people out of darkness. This is a statement that you hear and read about, but I would love to add to this truth. Angela Greenig loves to give other ministries opportunities to express their giftings and share the gospel of Jesus Christ. I find her, and her husband Larry, selfless acts worthy of being shared. I am honored that she has given River of Life Church the opportunity to share about our Deliverance & Healing Center. It was Angela who encouraged and trained us to stretch our ministry and move in this direction. Angela came in April 2014 to officially open our deliverance center. I am also honored to say that River of Life Church was her first deliverance center. It has been a great joy to see so many lives changed and transformed by the power and love of Jesus Christ.

JEANNIE and SHANE AMAR
Pastors, River of Life Church
Kentucky, USA
www.RiverofLifeKY.com

We have known Angela for more than ten years now. Her passion and commitment to see people saved, set free, and encounter God personally is contagious. Angela doesn't just preach the gospel, she demonstrates the gospel in power and anointing. All of her books and materials are full of revelation knowledge that is very pivotal to the times we are in. This book is especially relevant for those who need the reassurance that they have total victory over the enemy of their soul. Angela's life is a role model to so many of us who know her on a personal level. What you see in public ministry is what she lives every day as a true lover and follower of Christ.

PASTORS JOEL and JENNIFER CHUKS-NWOKIKE
Saving the Nations Ministry, Washington, USA
www.savingthenations.org

God is raising up a mighty army. He is calling the remnant to take their place as we march in unison to further God's Kingdom. This book is a powerful key for those engaging in spiritual warfare. Angela Greenig is truly a general in this army. The keys contained in this book are essential for such a time as this. God says in His Word, *"My people are destroyed for lack of knowledge"* (Hosea 4:6). This book will help to bring knowledge and understanding so the army of God can be victorious in the battle. Angela Greenig has been coming into our region for many years now training and equipping the body of Christ. Her ministry is unique and I have not seen another like it. I am honored to call her my friend.

PAMELA NEELY
Pastor, The Hub Church
Texas, USA

In her book, *Power and Authority Over Darkness,* Angela Greenig combines sound biblical principles with revelatory encounters to produce an invaluable foundational guide to spiritual warfare. Angela's book contains powerful revelation and wisdom from God that the body of Christ will appreciate. I have full confidence that anyone reading this book will experience greater freedom in their lives, even simply by praying the prayers Angela has written. I am thankful that God has raised up Angela for a time such as this to equip and raise up powerful spiritual warriors. Everyone should have a copy of this book on their bookshelf and read through it every once in a while.

RYAN LEE
Lead Pastor, Blessed International Revival Center
Anaheim, California, USA
www.blessedintl.com

If ever there was a time for the wisdom and insight on spiritual warfare found in this book, it is now. Forged in the fire of the Holy Spirit and trained on the front line of battle, no one is more qualified. Angela is a true warrior for the King of Kings who lives what she writes. A true friend who loves deeply, I am forever grateful for her encouragement and friendship. May this weapon set captives free and release soldiers into service to do what our Lord Jesus told us to do. Till the end.

BARBIE HUNT
Director, GATHER @ Main Street Prayer Center
Founder, Healing Rooms Kids
www.mainstreetprayer.org

When I first met Angela, I instantly felt that she was different. Different to be just who she is.

We need people like her. People who say what they think and speak what's on their heart with transparency and boldness. This will bring freedom into the church. Angela is like that. I'm reminded of the truth that our warfare is not against flesh and blood but against spiritual forces of evil, as taught to us in Ephesians 6:12—and this book makes it clearer than ever.

Several sentences stood out when I read *Power and Authority Over Darkness:* "The greatest trick the devil ever pulled was convincing the world he didn't exist." "Satan's biggest victory is that he made us believe he does not exist." "Make no mistake—we are at war! No general in the history of any nation has gone into combat without first finding out everything possible about those they are battling! That is how wars are won. The greatest battle strategy is to understand your opponent's strengths and weaknesses, then to amass an army whose greatest area of strength is their opponent's greatest area of weakness. But to do that, you must know your enemy." A general who is going into war tries to know as much as possible about the enemy to be victorious. This is, of course, also knowing your own arsenal that God gave you to win the battle. We are in this war together.

This book gives insight in how our enemy works in his ways to manipulate and deceive a generation that has been stolen from its God-given right to know what is going on. Angela is writing from her own experience, standing on this truth in Revelation 12:11 (AMP), *"And they overcame and conquered him…because of the word of their testimony, for they did not love their life and renounce their faith even when faced with death."* That test may as well be the future of the Western world church of today.

As well as we know that our Father's love is abiding in us every second of our lives, we also must know that we have a war to fight and to win. *Power and Authority Over Darkness* gives you faith and a new hunger to join in the battle—with joy. It makes you more aware and victorious for now and days to come. This book is a wake-up call carrying a truth that stands out among all. The devil is defeated and we need to live in that victory. This book is about that.

Angela is a ground-breaker and there was an immediate "click" between us when we had a couple of days together here in Sweden. We truly love her.

ULF CHRISTIANSSON
The House, Gothenburg, Sweden

POWER &
AUTHORITY
over DARKNESS

POWER &
AUTHORITY
over DARKNESS

HOW TO IDENTIFY & DEFEAT
16 EVIL SPIRITS
THAT WANT TO DESTROY YOU

ANGELA GREENIG

DESTINY IMAGE® PUBLISHERS, INC.
P.O. Box 310, Shippensburg, PA 17257-0310
"Promoting Inspired Lives."

This book and all other Destiny Image and Destiny Image Fiction books are available at Christian bookstores and distributors worldwide.

Cover design by Eileen Rockwell
Interior design by Terry Clifton

For more information on foreign distributors, call 717-532-3040.
Reach us on the Internet: www.destinyimage.com.

ISBN 13 TP: 978-0-7684-5094-1
ISBN 13 eBook: 978-0-7684-5095-8
ISBN 13 HC: 978-0-7684-5097-2
ISBN 13 LP: 978-0-7684-5096-5

For Worldwide Distribution, Printed in the U.S.A.
1 2 3 4 5 6 7 8 / 23 22 21 20 19

DEDICATION

TO THOSE SLINGSHOT-TOTING WARRIORS OF GOD WHO WILL GO and face the giants, you know who you are. Grab extra stones—it's time to demolish the demonic strongholds that plague our land. They have kept many imprisoned and bound for too long. I speak to all my brothers and sisters who are POWs and MIAs (Prisoners of War and Missing in Action), it is time for them to be found, break free, and come home. The war is real, satan is real, and what has been unleashed is real! We must be the watchmen who are stationed on the walls—the prophetic forerunners who will see the greatest outpouring of the Holy Spirit than ever before.

These strongholds must be removed...or *we* will be! We must be ready and position ourselves at our battle stations together, shields linked, working side by side. These are not the days of Elijah—we are the Elijahs of our day! No more COWs (Causalities of War). Hold on, we are coming for you.

Helen Keller said, "The only thing worse than being blind is having sight but no vision." I agree!

And my speech and my preaching were not with persuasive words of human wisdom, but in demonstration of the Spirit and of power, that your faith should not be in the wisdom of men but in the power of God (1 Corinthians 2:4-5).

...the kingdom of heaven suffers violence, and the violent take it by force (Matthew 11:12).

CONTENTS

CALL TO ACTION

WE ARE TO WIELD OUR SHIELD OF FAITH HIGH AND GRIP FIRMLY onto the sword of the Spirit, battling upward as we take back stolen ground. This ground was forfeited to the enemy, whether out of fear, lack of purpose, laziness, or ignorance…but it can *be recovered!*

While awaiting the sound of the trumpet blowing, announcing Christ's return, do you hear the sound of sirens? It is a 911 call! The emergency sirens are sounding in response to the needs all around us that are reaching cataclysmic proportions. Death is everywhere—the stench of death that reaches the Father's nostrils. There are many who are lost and dying and have not yet tasted freedom, because much of the church is dying for lack of knowledge. He is rising up and preparing to release the unsung heroes to rally together and fight. *No longer* can we allow satan to dispossess—deprive, cheat us out of—our birthright.

> *But when someone stronger than he attacks and overpowers him, he robs him of all his armor on which he had relied and divides his [goods as] spoil* (Luke 11:22 AMP).

1

No longer can we allow the enemy to steal our lives. *No longer* can we stand by and deny what the Holy Word declares. *We must refuse* to hide, barely getting by, afraid of what society has become. *We must refuse* to beg for crumbs that fall beneath the table, when Jesus paid the price in full so that we may sit with Him at that beautiful banquet table.

Truly, if Gideon can change the world, so can we! (See Judges 6–8.) We must come out of our caves, listen to the Word, and pull down all demonic strongholds that raise themselves above Jesus. We all must sacrificially lay down our own agendas so we can humbly and lovingly pick up His. Amen!

THE DREAM

I WAS LAUNCHED INTO DELIVERANCE MINISTRY BECAUSE OF A dream I had one night. This is the dream that propelled me into my destiny and prepared me for the unfolding of what was to take place. It was the first in a series of dreams and visions. Although it was many years ago, it is still so vivid to this day, and keeps me anchored in the fight to see souls delivered from the kingdom of darkness. I believe the dream was a divine setup from the Father to give me a hunger to see souls set free from the darkness, the fear, and the resulting pain. He used it to prepare me for what I'm doing today, and I am forever grateful. When you know that you know you are in the perfect will of God, you can endure many things. While these things are not always easy, He truly does go before us making the path straight and smooth.

This was the dream God gave me all those years ago:

> I was on the most incredible beach with a calm, warm breeze blowing, and I stopped for just a second to shut my eyes. The beauty and peace of my environment was

surreal and the sound of children at play reached my ears. As I opened my eyes and looked up, expecting to see children laughing and having fun, instead I saw only one boy, about of 9 or 10 years of age, sitting in a lounge chair. He was fully dressed and his eyes and hair were pitch black.

I was unsettled, but not afraid; as I drew closer to him, I began to feel sick to my stomach. Something was deeply wrong, and as I looked around, I saw many more people coming close. The people gathering were normal, everyday people: teachers, doctors, business-people, mothers, and fathers. They came nearer. The more I looked at them—through spiritual eyes and insight, rather than the natural—the more I began to see demons in their faces as they looked at me. They were hardly human anymore; the façade of normality receded, and they looked warped and twisted, even possessed.

As much as I wanted to run away and flee this horrible scene, I knew I had to wait to see what was next. The devil's voice began to speak to them with seductive and enticing false promises, and the crowd was utterly enthralled and captivated by his speech. As the joyful sounds of playing children morphed into torturous screams of pain and abuse, I knew the next step I took toward the crowd would be a hard one. But the step had to be taken.

All of a sudden, the earth opened up, and I could see what was going on. It appeared as if hell itself had been fully exposed. I saw the people screaming and on fire, swimming in a lake of fire. I saw silhouettes of people; all I could see was their faces as I thought to myself, *That could have been me.*

I knew I needed to help these people, and that's why I was hesitant to take that next step. I didn't know what it would mean if I did, and I wasn't sure if the earth was going to open up wider and swallow me as well. I had a strange presence come around me; and as I looked to my left and to my right, my two angels were with me, Bubba and Frank, and I knew in that moment that I would be okay! Once I took that step to help those who are trapped and heading to hell, I knew it was my calling and my only choice.

When the dream was over, I jumped quickly out of bed—it felt like my heart was coming out of my chest! I could barely breathe, I was so overwhelmed, I knew I was in a crazy dream of pure darkness. Honestly, I was scared to death, but I didn't understand the fullness of what the dream meant. I was under my dining room table for three days, praying and trying to understand what was going on. What did I need to do next?

ON THE THIRD DAY

I knew on the third day what had to be done, and I'm still doing it to this very day. I am to be a voice for those who have no voice, a defender for truth and justice, and to restore the paths of those back to the Father's true heart. I had a surge of confidence after praying into what this dream meant. It reminded me of the television show *Star Trek,* like being beamed up and transported somewhere otherworldly. I felt a beam of fire shooting through my bones, my entire being.

For the first time in my life I knew who I was, and I was comfortable with being myself. I began to speak the Word, and I told the devil he cannot have any of the souls I saw in my dream. I didn't feel the need to argue with him for long—I just kept saying the same thing over and over and over again, "By the blood of Jesus, you must let them go! By the blood of Jesus, by the blood of Jesus, by the blood of Jesus!" It was as if the more I said it, the more people kept walking across the chasm from hell to Jesus.

On the surface, everything can look perfect in people's lives. They appear to have it all together and have a measure of pleasure. We can never underestimate what is below the surface of appearance or what goes on behind closed doors. People mask their pain in many ways. As you look into the eyes of a person, you can get clearer insight to what is going on below the surface, and can speak life and love into the person. Before I learned what true freedom was, I myself was there many times before—held hostage by my own pain and fear when I believed lies about myself and my circumstances. In retrospect, when it is over, these people will literally be in hell forever if we do not speak the love of God to them. It would be a scary thing to stand before the Father and give an account as to why we did not tell them about Him and His love.

So my plea to you is, "Go, and do not look back!" Run into the fire and bring them out! When I did just that, I believe at that moment my life was changed forever. I thought about Peter getting out of the boat and walking on the water (Matthew 14:27-31). As he took a step of faith, he did not know what he was going to do, whether he was going to walk securely, or sink and drown. To see through our natural eyes, our own understanding and perception, this is what it would look like, but in the spiritual realm, that's not what happened. God took an impossible situation and made a possible one.

This story about Peter gave me the encouragement I needed to take that step, knowing my life would never be the same. Since that day, it never has. There will be times when you may second-guess yourself, not sure if you should get out of that boat and walk on the water, but be assured that whatever God is calling you to do, He will equip you to do it! I think sometimes we believe that all of the details, wisdom, and power we need will come to us all at once, or that everything will go according to our own plans. While that is the case sometimes, other times we must simply trust the Lord's prompting and go. He will provide what we need along the journey, and often uses the steps we take along the path to help us learn, grow, and move into our destiny.

Chapter 1

A LITTLE ABOUT ME

I WAS BORN IN 1958. I WAS AN ILLEGITIMATE CHILD, AS MY PARENTS were both married to other people. They had an affair, conceived me, divorced their current spouses, and eventually married each other. For the first twenty-one years of my life, I had a lot of confusion, was in a lot of pain, and had many problems. I was abused and not wanted by my mother's family, feeling the sting of rejection. At the age of 4, I had my first encounter with sexual abuse, which led me down a dark path and brought such a sense of shame. I had a very difficult time just being a child, and I can remember from early on the hurt, rejection, and abuse I was forced to endure. In school I was teased and bullied by other kids; I really struggled with a victim spirit, which preys on the weak.

In my childhood, I often wished I was dead as a way to end the pain I felt. My teachers in school were not caring and no help, saying aloud that I was stupid and would never amount to anything. Sadly, that's exactly what happened. Their words became declarations and became self-fulfilling prophecies, eventually leading me to drop out of school, which only caused additional problems. I believed the lie of the enemy that I was cursed to fail, destined to be worthless.

Growing up in a big family made it hard to survive mentally and financially. The stress of living with many people all dealing with their own major problems led to us projecting our issues onto one another and causing rifts in our household. The financial hardships of not always having basic needs met—much less wants—added to the anxiety. As an escape and a way to earn money for my family, I started dealing drugs in fourth grade. This went on for several years, opening the door to people and situations that were not in the best interest of a 9-year-old child. My parents eventually separated and then divorced, which is when the sadness, fear, and rejection took me into a downward spiral. I got deep into drugs, drinking, etc., basically you name it, and I did it. By the time I was 17, I began stripping in clubs, which quickly led me into prostitution. With such an unhealthy view of sex coming from an abusive childhood, as well as chemical and alcohol abuse, it was just a matter of time.

Although I felt rejected by my mother's family, I had a relationship with my dad's side of the family. I felt warmth and knew they loved me the best way they could. Unfortunately, my relatives on my dad's side didn't provide me with the healthy and stable family support that most children have, as my grandfather ran with the Italian mafia, specifically overseeing the south side of New Jersey. Because he had family and friends within the most influential mob families, I found protection in some areas of my life through them. Even with some protection through our family's mob connections however, I was still veering down the path of self-destruction.

One time when I was on a drunken-binge while hitchhiking, I was abducted for what I believe was a sex-trafficking operation. This was when I cried out to God for the first time. I was not sure if God was even real, and if He was, would He listen? I remember screaming, "If You're real, help me!" He heard my cry, and I was rescued that day from my abductor. Even after being rescued, I still went on drinking binges, trying to drown the demons in my head. Unfortunately, no matter how much I drank, they persisted. The voices wanted me to kill myself.

Into my adult years I continued to have a problem with chemical dependency, especially alcohol. In the midst of being a full-time alcoholic, I got pregnant young and married a few months later. I lacked the stability needed to maintain a permanent address and got divorced while still drinking. This erratic behavior went on for years.

Darkness had a stronghold on me and would not let me go! I tried drowning the pain with alcohol and drugs, but nothing truly helped. I remember while growing up that we dabbled in the occult. When substance abuse wasn't enough to free me from my demons, I looked for any kind of dark power that would pull me out of what had happened to me. I wanted revenge. I was in a really dark place that I couldn't break free from. During that time my mother did the hardest, bravest thing she could do to show me she loved me— she called Child Protective Services (CPS) to report the unsafe environment my daughter was being raised in. CPS stepped in and removed my daughter when she was an infant. While I may have been angry with her at the time, I consider myself so blessed that Mom placed that phone call to CPS, as I was on a wild, self-destructive binge, which was not safe for my daughter or me.

After CPS came and took away my daughter, I was broken and even more desperate to be free. My mom stepped in and insisted I meet with her pastor. I went begrudging, and only as a way to show her and CPS that I was willing to do whatever it took to get my daughter back. That meeting changed my life. The pastor told me,

"God loves you!" My immediate response was thinking, *Love? As in sex?* It was obviously not that kind of love, but I honestly did not understand what love was, or what love outside of sex meant. My definition of love was not God's.

As the pastor shared about Jesus and His death on the cross, I felt warmth run all over my body, and tears started to stream down my face. For the first time in my life, when I looked around me, I didn't see any of the dark-winged ones; they were gone. The demons were gone! Instead, I saw a brilliant light. I could see colors, colors more brilliant than the rainbow.

LIFE TRANSPLANT

That day in a small office on August 13, 1980, there was a life transplant! I was saved! God's love and mercy broke the darkness off me, and I realized so much! I realized that God had always been there—through the pain, the fear, and the darkness. I had to find light within for Him to be able to shine upon me. I immediately made a 180° change and devoted my life to God and His work.

By dropping out in school, I was basically illiterate, but on my third day after encountering God in such a powerful way, I was able to read! I reached for my new Bible, randomly opened it, and there was Matthew 10:6-8, which said to go and tell others about the Kingdom of Heaven. To lay hands on the sick and they will be healed, and to bring in the lost...so that's what I did. I went out and started to share the love of Jesus with others, and several people were healed and saved that day. Those who knew the old me asked, "Oh my God! What has happened to you?" I told them, "God happened, and He is real!" I said, "You want some of this!?" (I'm a Jersey girl, after all). They did! So, we prayed. It was amazing to see people accept Christ, receive healing, and discover that His love is so immense for them!

God restored my heart, my family, and my whole life. There is no greater love than the one from our heavenly Father, and I truly want everyone to know that. We all have a powerful testimony, and this is just a small portion of mine. It is important to remember that God is not afraid of the stains and scars we bring to Him. He is a big God and is ready at any moment to breathe life, shed light, and show His love.

As I began to write my first book years later, the dream I had about the beach began to make sense to me. I know at times the Lord will give us a seemingly impossible prompting or potentially illogical instruction. What He shows or says seems to not make any sense. It might make no sense in the natural, but that's where faith comes in. He is faithful and trustworthy. When He declares something, it will come to pass. Romans 4:17 says to speak those things that are not as though they are, and in Jeremiah 1:12 that He will watch over His word. If we hold these promises deep in our hearts, we will see Him fulfill each one!

VISIONS OF WHAT WAS TO COME

September 11, 2001

I have been in the habit for many years of taking time out alone to pray. I refer to it as "lock down"—a time away from everything, fully engaged in fasting, prayer, and seeking the Lord. This particular lock down was specifically to pray into a date on the calendar that I felt the Lord placed into my spirit—that date was September 11. I felt like the Lord was urging me to draw away with Him starting on the ninth of September through the eleventh each year. In the beginning, I didn't understand why He asked me to commit to prayer during September ninth through the eleventh each year, but I understood clearly in 1999. It was then when I started having horrific visions of what was to come. It felt like being caught up in a jet stream in the spirit, amidst a myriad of sights and sounds! I would see fire and smoke, people in utter chaos, fear, death, sorrow, and great pain. It was like watching a movie unfold before my eyes, and I could not look away from it. I cried and cried, and knew for certain that something was going to happen—on September 11, 2001.

In 2001, the vision came again as I was preaching at two churches: one in Texarkana, Texas, in March, and the other in Nashville, Tennessee, in June. In the middle of each of my sermons, the Holy Spirit showed me the vision. What I saw in the vision was so horrible and devastating. Both times, I felt prompted to share aloud what I saw in the vision, and I heard from the Father that September 11, 2001, would be cataclysmic; the stench of burning flesh would reach into Heaven itself. I saw mayhem and chaos erupting. Something big was coming. I fell out of my chair in fear of what would take place. All the previous years I had committed myself to fasting and prayer during this three-day period were coming to a crescendo. I kept hearing an alarm over and over, a siren. Little did I know the full significance of the carnage that would occur.

On September 10, 2001, at 3:10 in the afternoon, our son, Chad, had arrived home from school. We started to pray, thanking God for a safe day at school, when I was immediately taken into the spirit realm. As I was lifted up, I saw the principality—a ruler over a territory, in this case demonic in nature—Babylon hovering over the east coast border of New Jersey and New York. I saw Babylon starting to methodically maneuver into position. Immediately I found myself observing the West Coast, where the Prince of Persia was waiting as well, pacing up and down the coast, planning something I was not sure of. I was so overwhelmed by what I saw in my vision!

A sound hit the airwaves. Hordes of demons were dispatched all over the United States. In cities across the nation, I saw what looked like manhole covers being blown off and exposing what had been hidden below the surface. As they were released, suddenly the Prince of Babylon and Prince of Persia took flight, their wing spans seemed to cover the entire country. As they flew closer to one another at a great speed, their swords clashed and clanged, emitting a dark gray cloud that looked like a smoke screen over Colorado. They were getting repositioned and exchanged their territorial authority—a changing of the guard moment.

The next day, New York City had been attacked and was engulfed in a thick gray cloud. Thousands of our beautiful brothers and sisters lost their lives. Was our military prepared for such extreme attacks and acts of violence on American soil? Yes, we were ready for the expected, but not prepared for an unleashing of this magnitude. There were four airplanes targeting three strategic locations. Each was strategically planned to weaken our financial (the Twin Towers), military (Pentagon), and governmental (White House or Capitol building) pillars. Our country appeared crippled from this attack, yet we are stronger now than ever before. *United we stand, divided we fall!*

The Prince of Persia had taken his position on the East Coast and revealed himself in the natural. News coverage across the country shared photos of a shadowy figure arising amidst the smoke and rubble, his face screaming in the smoke. Babylon had also repositioned itself, as Washington State and Oregon were hit devastatingly hard economically. Boeing, one of the major sources of industry in Washington State, was greatly affected with loss that cascaded down into areas of the smaller supporting companies. The domino effects from this attack were difficult to recover from. This is one example of how the spirit and natural realms coexist and are intertwined, and how changes to one affect the other. My life's lesson prepared me for the years still to come.

Earthquake in Turkey

In 2011, I was preaching down south in the United States, and a violent shaking hit my spirit. It came so swiftly that I fought to not convulse and fall over as I tried to hold myself upright, using the church's pulpit for leverage. Once again, a gripping took hold of me, and the Lord said to me, "Speak now." I ended up violently convulsing on the floor. I told the crowd, "I saw the number one gate, Turkey, and the gates were opened. 'There will be a quaking, and it will be a sign,' says the Lord. 'What once was won't be again.'"

In a matter of hours, I was contacted by my staff.

"Oh my gosh, Angela! There's been an earthquake!"

I said, "In Turkey?"

"Yes, in Turkey!"

I asked, "What was the Richter scale?"

"7.2."

I hung up the phone immediately and fell to my knees and began to pray, "Oh Lord, You wanted me to speak through the violent shaking of my body. You wanted me to say Turkey, the number one gate, would be a sign." I felt like my travailing on the floor was a direct parallel to the quaking that was happening in Turkey at that moment, and a reflection of what was going on in the supernatural.

As I look back, I didn't know then if I would make it. I went to people and sought answers to many questions about the things I saw, the time travel I would take, etc. I am a seer, which is someone who receives divine insight from Heaven in visions and dreams, who has the ability to tap into the mysteries and sights of the heavenly realms. Through the years, the Lord has been faithful to help me understand the gift He has given me as a seer, and I've come to embrace my gifts now, and not tweak about what I see—well, I should say not tweak as much. To know and see things that happen a lot is overwhelming at times. The visions are hard, but I know when I pray that God will move. I trust Him.

Both spiritually and in the natural, we must protect what God has given us. We must guard the gates of the Atlantic and Pacific coasts, mainly New York City and Los Angeles. In the early 1960s, we as a nation stopped telling people who came to live in America about our God, Jehovah, and that our country was founded on godly principles. We actually used to give a Bible to new citizens when they arrived. This was also around the same time that prayer started being removed from our public schools! More than forty years have passed—forty represents testing—and we don't have another forty years to waste. We are on a timeline trying to follow a plumb line to redeem our land and see right alignment brought to it. We must fight against the injustice that has become a cancer in our land. It is not too late; we still have time!

The requests the Lord makes of us are like seeds. We can choose to agree and partner with the Lord to see the seed flourish, or we can choose to dismiss it or let someone else destroy the seed with their words. No matter how big or small the seed is that the Lord has planted in your spirit, protect it, pursue it, and see it to fruition. If God has called you to do it, every bit of provision you need will be supplied, every bit of boldness and strength and resources. There is no greater "backer" than the King of the universe!

Here we are again today, years later, still experiencing wars and rumors of war. We must allow urgency to arise in our spirits and see that time is running out. We must prepare. Now is the appointed time. Heaven's courtroom has a mandate—execute judgment against the ungodly acts that go on every day in every nation. We have been chosen to be voices and to go and be witnesses of

His power and carriers of His glory to a lost and very dark world. Arise and shine for His light has come, and it's in each one of us. "Be strong and of a good courage; be not afraid, for I am with you wherever you go," says the Lord.

May His truth encourage you and equip you, reminding you just how powerful God has created you to be. We must recognize the signs that are all around us. You are a vital part of God's plan to see His Kingdom come to earth! If not you, then who? If not now, then when? As watchmen, we must be at our post guarding and protecting the gateways to our neighborhoods, cities, and nations.

PRAYER

Father, we release Heaven's host of angels to move on our behalf. We decree Psalm 103:19-22 (AMP):

The Lord has established His throne in the heavens, and His sovereignty rules over all [the universe]. Bless the Lord, you His angels, you mighty ones who do His commandments, obeying the voice of His word! Bless the Lord, all you His hosts, you who serve Him and do His will. Bless the Lord, all you works of His, in all places of His dominion; bless and affectionately praise the Lord, O my soul!

Chapter 2

FAITH FOR FREEDOM

FREEDOM: The state of being free or at liberty, rather than in confinement or under physical restraint; exemption from external control, interference, regulation, etc.; personal liberty, as opposed to bondage or slavery.

FREEDOM WILL COST YOU EVERYTHING!

To understand, and begin to really walk in the fullness of freedom afforded to us by our faith, we need not only understand freedom itself, but must also recognize and actively seek liberty from our former bondage. In His death and resurrection, our great King and High Priest Jesus Christ made full provision for total victory and absolute freedom in every area of our lives. Because this provision has already been made, and because in the Holy Spirit we have everything pertaining to life and godliness, then why do so many of us struggle with old sins and old ways of thinking and doing?

The grace of God is a free gift; like any gift it must be received, and to be received it first has to be believed! So many believers are living far beneath the call of God on their lives simply because they are ignorant of the extravagantly precious inheritance we have as saints—as sons and daughters of the Most High God. It has been said that Jesus came not only to get us into Heaven, but to get Heaven into us! Our salvation, the moment our names are written in the book of life, is only the very beginning of a lifelong journey into the progressive revelation of the true nature of our God and the things of His Kingdom.

Cultivating an ever-deepening intimacy with God is the primary call of our lives as followers of Christ. To know Him better today than yesterday, and to love Him and honor Him in all things, not out of a sense of obligation or compunction, but out of the overwhelming joy of communing and worshipping Him in spirit and truth. As we learn to seek first His kingship and His righteousness, all the rest will follow. But when we seek Him and His Kingdom for the sake of all that follows, we are no longer really seeking Him first, we are seeking His blessings. Knowing Him is its own reward, and there is no other blessing or benefit that comes close to it. When we seek Him with reckless abandon and learn to trust Him deeper and deeper, things begin to change radically for the better—for His glory and for our benefit.

As believers, we live in the tension between two realities. The more readily apparent of these realities is the place we live and the ugliness we see and experience on a day-to-day basis, but the greater reality we have the opportunity of living from is the truth of our Father's Kingdom. Second Corinthians 4:18 says, *"While we do not look at the things which are seen, but at the things which are not seen. For the things which are seen are temporary, but the things which are not seen are eternal."* It takes absolutely zero faith to partner with the reality presented by this fallen world. Without believing in and partnering with God's truth, we become beaten down and hopeless in the face of hardship; futility sets in, and we give up. We allow the way people treat us to define our worth and value and grow bitter and resentful toward them. The flame of our childhood hopes and dreams grow cold, and we find our lives small and empty.

Apart from God, the only way to overcome the cycle is to take on the yoke of this material world and find our pleasure and purpose in petty comforts and selfish ambition. We begin chasing riches, creature comforts, or worldly achievements and prestige, which only develop an ever-increasing appetite for what the world has to offer. This appetite becomes more and more ravenous without offering true satisfaction. People who climb the world's ladder in their own strength can only make it so far before they end up needing to defraud and harm other people to successfully satisfy their now-darkened desires.

To partner with Kingdom reality is to unwaveringly believe in who God is, what He has already done, and what He wants to do. We must truly know what His heart is toward us. God is sovereign, and He has ways of accomplishing His will with or without our participation. At the same time, God has trusted us to partner and co-labor with Him in bringing His light and hope to the darkened world around us. In fact, all of creation groans in anticipation for the children of God to realize their inheritance and bring His Kingdom here! Jesus did not ask us for a confession of faith and a Sunday morning spent in a building—He asked us for our very selves. He wants our whole lives laid down in a trusting surrender to His mercy, love, and goodness. *"Whoever finds their life will lose it, and whoever loses their life for my sake will find it"* (Matthew 10:39 NIV).

As we learn to trust and surrender to Him, He provides us with joy, peace, and hope such as nothing in the world can offer. He does not change the world around us; He changes us and empowers *us* to change our world. This is a much greater glory than if He just swooped in and did all the work Himself. We have the honor and privilege of learning and growing in the works that we see our Father doing—He asks only that we believe.

The final hindrance to God's will being accomplished in our lives and across the earth, and the subject of the book, is this: God has an enemy who hates Him, and therefore hates us. Satan is real; and while he can never truly win or accomplish any lasting victory over God, he is content to hijack people, destroy goodness, and rob people of knowing God for as long as possible. The devil is the commander-in-chief over an entire kingdom of darkness, and he mobilizes his minions to kill, steal, and destroy at every opportunity. Jesus came to destroy the works of darkness, and since we are called to walk as He walked, it should be our top priority to war against the powers of hell.

OUR GOD OF JUSTICE

A believer who has studied the Old Testament knows that our God is a God of justice, of vengeance, of wrath, and of war. A common misconception in many streams of today's faith is that since Jesus came and nullified the power of sin, God is no longer zealous to execute His judgment on darkness. Jesus forever changed the relationship between God and humankind so that the Father now sees us as sons and daughters, and no longer demands continual atonement for sin.

Jesus really did pay it all, and we will spend all of our time here and hereafter thanking and praising Him for His mercy! However, being that God is the same yesterday, today, and forever, we can trust that all the aspects of God revealed in the Old Testament are just as true and active as ever. Yes, our God is kind and gentle. He is an endlessly patient and loving Father. But He is still the God of all justice and will exact vengeance on His adversary. It may seem to us that justice and mercy are at odds and cannot coexist, but in Him they are always in perfect harmony. Jesus the Lamb is revealed to us in the gospels; Jesus the Lion is revealed in Revelation. And we are closer to the end than the beginning.

"The greatest trick the devil ever pulled was convincing the world he didn't exist." This quote may be from the movie *The Usual Suspects,* but the truth in this statement is absolutely on target. The devil is real, and he has many names. This book, *Power and Authority Over Darkness,* is intended to serve as a resource to help dispel the lies of the enemy, proving once again, through the Holy Spirit and God's Word, that satan does in fact exist, as does his army.

> *One day the angels came to present themselves before the Lord, and Satan also came with them. The Lord said to Satan, "Where have you come from?" Satan answered the Lord, "From roaming throughout the earth, going back and forth on it"* (Job 1:6-7 NIV).

Satan still exists today, roaming the earth to and fro, planting seeds of deception in his wake of destruction. He is the accuser of believers, undoubtedly, but take heart! Our intercession can and will cancel him out!

> *Be sober [well balanced and self-disciplined], be alert and cautious at all times. That enemy of yours, the devil, prowls around like a roaring lion [fiercely hungry], seeking someone to devour* (1 Peter 5:8 AMP).

Make no mistake—we are at war! No general in the history of any nation has gone into combat without first finding out everything they possibly can about those they are battling! That is how wars are won. The greatest battle strategy is to understand your opponent's strengths and weaknesses, then to amass an army whose greatest area of strength is their opponent's greatest area of weakness. But to do that, you must know your enemy.

The ministry the Lord called me to establish—Set Free Ministries and Angela Greenig Ministries—believes we have been called to assist God's people in receiving the healing and training to be fully equipped to overcome the enemy and see God's land restored. We have received a mandate from the Lord to rise up reconnaissance stations as well as deliverance and healing centers. We are also called to serve as spiritual watchmen on an outpost, helping serve the body of Christ by sharing what the Lord reveals to us on the horizon from our watchtowers.

We have an army waiting to be released, to usher in this next great wave of His glory—it's time for the greatest revival ever! Many will be saved in this revival, predominantly those in the occult.

> *As I looked, thrones were set in place, and the Ancient of Days took his seat. His clothing was as white as snow; the hair of his head was white like wool. His throne was flaming with fire, and its wheels were all ablaze. A river of fire was flowing, coming out from before him. Thousands upon thousands attended him; ten thousand times ten thousand stood before him. The court was seated, and the books were opened* (Daniel 7:9-10 NIV).

A violent outpouring of His glory has already transcended! It's time for the Ancient of Days to take His seat of authority within each one of our hearts! We are on a prophetic time clock, and it is tick...tick...ticking. In 2006 we celebrated 100 years since the Azusa Street revival in Los Angeles, California. The Lord spoke to me and said, "You are part of the generation that will take this power and release My end-time army!" This outbreak would start to take place within these next three years. The heavens have been opened with an unleashing of the greatest miracles, signs, and wonders *ever!*

We are the true ark-bearers, carriers of His glory, and we will embark on a new frontier. But just as those who came to America from England in search of freedom, we too, must etch out the moral dealings and take back what we have lost. If we could only see who we really are, with the dominion and power that reigns in each one of us, we would be armed and dangerous!

> *Now faith is confidence in what we hope for and assurance about what we do not see* (Hebrews 11:1 NIV).

John Wimber said that faith is spelled R-I-S-K. I have always felt like faith is for things present, and hope is for the things to come. As we believe, we will see God move. Now we know the Bible says that faith without works is dead (James 2:17). So, while it is very important to have faith in our hearts and spirits, there is going to be some work that must accompany our faith. This may also come in the way of a little pruning and polishing by the Father, but the finished result will make us like gold. This refining means our minds must continually be washed by the Word, the Bible, and we must continue taking steps toward holiness, wholeness, loving, serving, etc.

No Stinking (Negative) Thinking!

> *And do not be conformed to this world, but be transformed by the renewing of your mind, that you may prove*

what is that good and acceptable and perfect will of God
(Romans 12:2).

We must allow God to move in and through us, and that can often mean embracing change. By aligning ourselves with the Word of God, we become like Him, and that is where true transformation comes. During more than thirty years of ministry, we have seen multitudes of people saved, healed, delivered, and set free. I believe the Father has taught me so many valuable lessons through the numerous deliverances and healings that our ministry has been able to bring to God's people. With deliverance and healing centers throughout the United States and in many nations, we are growing stronger in our crusade for freedom and healing. More and more believers are hearing the call of the Lord and are stepping up in faith to actively fight against the darkness. We are winning!

Each of us are covered by God's grace and love through Jesus' sacrifice, and these already guarantee us victory. I do not have to fight for victory, as that has already been achieved through the cross, and each of us has access to that victory. Amen! Now we simply get the privilege of walking out that victory in our personal lives, and helping others receive their same inheritance of victory.

Walking out our victory is a daily, intentional pursuit, and I keep pressing on to the higher call I know He has for my life. It is my greatest privilege to know that the Lord has given me keys to help teach and train up the end-time army of warriors, true soldiers of the cross who are called to illuminate His light and edge out the darkness, one soul at a time.

Claiming our victory means walking in the truth written in Scripture that helps us understand our true identity as His saints. We are children of the God of Heaven and earth, made in His image, and healed by the stripes of His Son who laid His life down for each one of us. This requires us to not only have thoughts in our mind that align with the truth in God's Word, but also the words we speak. Words are powerful! When we speak, we create and set boundaries for our lives. If our words are shallow or not aligned with truth, we may find our boundaries are limiting us from the fullness Christ intended for us. Words are like arrows, and they will find their target. I urge you to be careful of the things you speak, for they go into the airwaves and will return to you.

Remember that satan is the prince of the air and hears what you speak. He takes great pleasure in trying to manipulate and pervert what is positive, while using the negative against you. Have faith that God will turn situations that appear to be bad into good, and speak positive confessions concerning the outcome of situations, even if they haven't come to pass yet. Speaking further about life and death and the power of words, we get to choose. Will we choose life or death?

> *Death and life are in the power of the tongue, and those who love it will eat its fruit* (Proverbs 18:21).

We are a three-part being: spirit, soul, and body. Our soul is comprised of our mind, will, and emotions. When we are attacked by satan, it is usually in one of three ways: physical, mental, or emotional. Remember, we have a free will and we consciously make choices. So, will we succumb to the devil's schemes and allow him to redefine our destinies? Or will we take the authority given to us through the Father to resist the devil, confident that the Word of God says he must flee?

We have been created to have a relationship with God. Relationship is defined as being connected; kinship; being connected by blood or marriage; a continuing attachment or association between persons. We must be like the woman with the issue of blood

(Mark 5:25-34) and press in to receive our miracles. Please don't allow physical, emotional, or mental challenges to keep you from a passionate pursuit of the Lord. The condition of our "feelings" has kept many of God's people bound and spiritually hemorrhaging.

LIVE A FULL-MEASURE LIFE

God has given you authority to manage your soul—mind, will, emotions—which means that your soul does not have the power to dictate to you. Unfortunately, so many people don't realize that and live their lives stuck between two thieves—the past and the future. The thief of their past tells them they are disqualified because of what they've done. The thief of their future tells them they can never be more than they are today and to give up on hope.

As I began to write this morning, I thought to myself, *Ange, you must persevere and press through. You have to get this book done or you cannot move on to the next few books that are waiting to be compiled and completed. You have intel on the enemy that many don't have. You have a responsibility to help those people.* So, I spoke life into my soul and kept writing. The reason I mention this is simple: Do we really want to look back on our lives and see how wonderful they could have been if we were not afraid to live them fully? Whatever a full-measure life may look like to you, remember that it is never too late.

For me, a fulfilled life is sharing the message of freedom to the captives through television, books, and preaching the gospel worldwide. It is a lot of work when there are only a few people doing the work; but when we are all moving together in the flow of God's river, being who He uniquely called us each to be, the work becomes light and His gospel begins to spread like wildfire. So, I urge you to pray and to believe in the call on your life; take back what belongs to you!

The Hebrew word for faith is *emunah*, which means trust, faithful, stable, and steady. The word for faith in Greek is *pistis*, which means assurance, to believe, be confident in, rely on, or faith to confidently believe. One of the biggest thieves of faith in our lives is compromise. While compromise feels like a solution because it "meets in the middle," there is no room for compromise when it comes to the truths of God. Compromise will eat away at your faith, and your confidence, often leaving you weary and tired. That is why it is so important to stir up the gifts you have been given by God and allow Him to have your heart freely and completely. I've found that putting my faith into action more than twenty-five years ago was key for me, and recalling these principles is still how I personally stay the course in my personal life.

It is also important to pay attention to the company you keep. I like this wonderful quote, "Show me your friends, and I'll show you your future." I love everyone, but I am an eagle not a chicken. I can't be cooped up barely getting by, crying about what once was and now it's not. I fly with those of like minds—many of whom have forged ahead, paid the price, and have wisdom and revelation. I need that. Movers and shakers.

HOW TO PUT YOUR FAITH INTO ACTION

Stay in the Word.

Jesus rebutted each of satan's words using the living word. We are to do the same. Romans 12:2 (AMP) says:

> *And do not be conformed to this world [any longer with its superficial values and customs], but be transformed and progressively changed [as you mature spiritually] by the renewing of your mind [focusing on godly values and ethical attitudes], so that you may prove [for yourselves]*

what the will of God is, that which is good and acceptable
and perfect [in His plan and purpose for you].

Confess positively.

Proverbs 18:21 (NIV) speaks about how life and death are in
the power of the tongue, and those who love it and indulge in it
will eat its fruit, and bear the consequences of their words: *"The*
tongue has the power of life and death, and those who love it will eat
its fruits." Remember that quote from Andy Rooney, "Always keep
your words soft and sweet, just in case you have to eat them."

Act on the Word.

James 1:19-22 (AMP) says:

> *Understand this, my beloved brothers and sisters.*
> *Let everyone be quick to hear [be a careful, thoughtful*
> *listener], slow to speak [a speaker of carefully chosen words*
> *and], slow to anger [patient, reflective, forgiving]; for*
> *the [resentful, deep-seated] anger of man does not produce*
> *the righteousness of God [that standard of behavior which*
> *He requires from us]. So get rid of all uncleanness and*
> *all that remains of wickedness, and with a humble spirit*
> *receive the word [of God] which is implanted [actually*
> *rooted in your heart], which is able to save your souls. But*
> *prove yourselves doers of the word [actively and contin-*
> *ually obeying God's precepts], and not merely listeners*
> *[who hear the word but fail to internalize its meaning],*
> *deluding yourselves [by unsound reasoning contrary to the*
> *truth].*

Learn and memorize Scripture.

Learning and memorizing Scripture is vital; it's how we renew
our minds. *"So then faith comes by hearing, and hearing by the word*

of God" (Romans 10:17). Some people have the Word and worship music playing 24/7. To stay filled, I personally have worship music playing all the time. It helps me to connect and abide in the Father more than I can say.

Pray God's presence.

We do not have to beg, as we have access to His Spirit. Those who are led by the Spirit walk by the Spirit. *"And the Spirit of the Lord will rest on Him, the Spirit of wisdom and understanding, the Spirit of counsel and strength, the Spirit of knowledge and of the [reverential and obedient] fear of the Lord"* (Isaiah 11:2 AMP). In the spiritual realm, the flow of the prophetic from Heaven to earth is like two streams coming together. As these streams meet, it is like a collision, forming different degrees or dimensions. With so much stirring in the spirit (whether we can see it or not), it makes our connection to God even more important, so we can discern those degrees or dimensions when they are revealed to us. As we read in Isaiah 11, to be led by the Spirit of God means we must walk in the spirit. To walk in the spirit is to place ourselves on the path of what God is doing in the spiritual realm and follow it. His presence is a gateway to getting ourselves on the path.

Pray for the fear of the Lord to be active in your life.

The fear of the Lord is not like most of us interpret fear. Fear of the Lord is one of reverence and respect for who He is. It is not a fear intended to rule over you or force you to do His bidding. The fear of the Lord is the key that enables us to obey Him: *"The fear of the Lord is the beginning of wisdom, and the knowledge of the Holy One is understanding"* (Proverbs 9:10 NIV).

Pray for divine wisdom and understanding.

As we get closer to Him, we learn to hear His voice clearer. Ask Him how to apply what He's speaking to you. We are made wiser as God builds us up in the understanding of Him. As He gives understanding, you will understand the paths He is calling you to walk on: *"For I will give you a mouth and wisdom which all your adversaries will not be able to contradict or resist"* (Luke 21:15).

Pray for confidence.

Pray for confidence to be who He's created you to be, and to receive that inheritance.

> *In Him also we have received an inheritance [a destiny—we were claimed by God as His own], having been predestined* (chosen, appointed beforehand) *according to the purpose of Him who works everything in agreement with the counsel and design of His will, so that we who were the first to hope in Christ [who first put our confidence in Him as our Lord and Savior] would exist to the praise of His glory* (Ephesians 1:11-12 AMP).

Chapter 3

FRUIT INSPECTION

In Matthew 7:20, Jesus uses trees to share a very important analogy about discernment. He said, *"You will know them by their fruits."* Whether good or evil, the fruit exhibited in someone's life should show you a glimpse into the health of the person's soul.

With every tree there is good or bad fruit. For example, when people are drunk all of the time and can't stop drinking, well… you know they have a problem. They are bound by alcohol. It has a hold on them. It can devastate their health, family, work, and many aspects of their lives. While it is easy to label people as "drunks," what we actually see is the bad fruit on the branches of their lives, which is the by-product of a broken person that satan lied to, seduced, and bound.

Sometimes the fruit of a person's life is so deceptive that you can't see the wolf in sheep's clothing. This may sound discouraging, but is actually meant to encourage you. With the help of the Holy Spirit, you will learn to discern when someone has an inner battle raging, and you can use the weapons discussed in this book to help bring that person into freedom.

One of the greatest battles people have, and allow themselves to be held back by, is *doubt*. Once we break through the barrier of doubt, we can help lead others into total freedom. Statistics say that 89 percent of people are not happy with their lives. Are you happy? What holds you back from your full potential? If I had to guess, I would say it is the opinions of others about you, and your opinion of yourself. These are the situations you need to deal with. Let me tell you this: once you do, your life is never the same.

I am reminded of Matthew 13:1-23, the parable about the sower, the seed, and the ground. Seeds fell along the path, the rocky ground, the thorns, and good soil. It is so important that we are wise stewards over our souls and are pliable when the Lord is looking to plant truth into our hearts. Alternately, it is equally important that we guard our hearts and minds from outside factors that would try and snatch those seeds of truth and replace them with lies, discouragement, and doubt.

Psalm 1 speaks about how our roots need to be deeply planted in the Lord, the Word, and in our relationship to our family. When the waters of life's troubles arise, if our roots are not deeply planted in God, the things that have grown will wither and could eventually die. Guard your heart and protect those roots: *"He shall be like a tree planted by the rivers of water, that brings forth its fruit in its season, whose leaf also shall not wither; and whatever he does shall prosper"* (Psalm 1:3).

A GREAT DAY!

Every day, I wake up and say, "Good morning, Lord. It's going to be a great day!" I know He's going to fill me up with good stuff, and my cup will overflow with blessings, miracles, signs, wonders, grace, and love. I have assurance that He will reach and impact my life as well as those I come in contact with. The first thought I choose to have each day is to place God first.

Did you know that 2,400 times a day our minds are bombarded with troublesome thoughts? Granted, I understand when we've gone through horrific trials, death, loss of a job, or when our children are in trouble, these weigh heavily on our minds. I have learned to keep fighting off futility. We have the opportunity to speak life or death into each situation, as the power in our tongue speaks volumes. We do not have to go by what we see, feel, or hear—we can choose to live by the Living Word of God.

In my quiet times with the Father, there are several things I offer to Him and speak over my life daily that help me align my day with His heart and with what is best for me. I offer Him and speak over my life:

Praise and worship (to glorify). I offer Him my thankfulness for who He is to me, often through prayers and songs. I sing a lot, no matter where I am or what time of day. *"I will worship toward Your holy temple, and praise Your name for Your lovingkindness and Your truth; for You have magnified Your word above all Your name"* (Psalm 138:2).

My heart and plans (to partner). The Lord knows our hearts, but still wants to be invited into the conversation. *"My heart rejoices in the Lord; my horn is exalted in the Lord. I smile at my enemies, because I rejoice in Your salvation"* (1 Samuel 2:1).

My filthy rags, and "put on" Jesus (to renew). I remove what separates me from Him and robe myself in Him, making me more like Him. *"Therefore put to death your members which are on the earth: fornication, uncleanness, passion, evil desire, and covetousness, which is idolatry"* (Colossians 3:5). *"But now you yourselves are to put off all these: anger, wrath, malice, blasphemy, filthy language out of your mouth"* (Colossians 3:8). We have to take off the past, the old person. *"Therefore, as the elect of God, holy and beloved, put on tender mercies, kindness, humility, meekness, longsuffering"* (Colossians 3:12).

Pray for a heart of love (to serve). Charity is love, and love never fails. The Lord exalts a Christlike character more than ministries, positions, titles, or spiritual gifts. He is all the goodness in our lives—the gifts and fruit and life. Love is the greatest, most powerful weapon we have to defeat the enemy every time. Love never fails. *"Though I speak with the tongues of men and of angels, but have not love, I have become sounding brass or a clanging cymbal"* (1 Corinthians 13:1). And First Corinthians 13:13 (AMP) says, *"And now there remain: faith [abiding trust in God and His promises], hope [confident expectation of eternal salvation], love [unselfish love for others growing out of God's love for me], these three [the choicest graces]; but the greatest of these is love."*

Fruit of the Holy Spirit. I pray for the fruits of the Spirit to increase in my life every day. I love First Corinthians 13. I have learned one thing, Jesus desires a Christlike character more than the giftings. Why? Because He is the gift and we choose to be inhabited by a Christlike character.

"But the fruit of the Spirit is love, joy, peace, longsuffering, kindness, goodness, faithfulness, gentleness, self-control. Against such there is no law" (Galatians 5:22-23).

Galatians 5:22-23 is a well-known and loved passage of Scripture, but I feel people often gloss over the significance of each fruit of the Spirit represented in these two verses. Each one is distinct and valuable, and to incorporate these fruits into our daily lives is so important to living life to the full.

Let's take a deeper look into each fruit of the Holy Spirit:

Love. Love is wanting the best for someone with no personal motive or gain intended, just pure love. This truth is such a deep revelation! It is a definition worth reading a few times. This is the heartbeat and mandate of my ministry. I'm often asked, "Angela, what do you think is your greatest weapon?" My response is always the same, love. Many times, my answer produces a puzzled look. Folks expect something tactical, but without love there is nothing. Love is the greatest weapon in my arsenal. *"Above all these things put on love, which is the bond of perfection"* (Colossians 3:14). When we have been hurt, we must respond like Christ. I read over this passage, allowing Him to replace my thoughts with His. This takes time.

Joy. Joy is great gladness based on His love for others. I love seeing the joy of the Lord impact the lives of pre-believers. *"I will delight myself in Your statutes; I will not forget Your word"* (Psalm 119:16).

Peace. There is peace when the heart and mind are aligned from a vibrant relationship with the Lord. *"You have put gladness in my heart, more than in the season that their grain and wine increased"* (Psalm 4:7).

Longsuffering (patience). To be patient is to be slow to anger, representing a renewed strength of mind. *"And do not be conformed to this world, but be transformed by the renewing of your mind, that you may prove what is that good and acceptable and perfect will of God"* (Romans 12:2).

Kindness. Kindness is doing good to all people and not wanting to hurt anyone. *"And be kind to one another, tenderhearted, forgiving one another, even as God in Christ forgave you"* (Ephesians 4:32).

Goodness. Goodness is to walk in truth and kindness, also rebuking evil and correcting to produce truth and kindness. *"Then Jesus went into the temple of God and drove out all those who bought and sold in the temple, and overturned the tables of the money changers and the seats of those who sold doves. And He said to them, 'It is* written, *"My house shall be called a house of prayer,"* but you have made it a *"den of thieves""* (Matthew 21:12-13).

Faithfulness. Being faithful is to be loyal, committed, and trustworthy. *"For what if some did not believe? Shall their unbelief make the faithfulness of God without effect?"* (Romans 3:3). *"What then? If some did not believe or were unfaithful [to God], their lack of belief will not nullify and make invalid the faithfulness of God and His word, will it? Certainly not! Let God be found true [as He will be], though every person be found a liar, just as it is written [in Scripture], "That you may be justified in your words, and prevail when you are judged [by sinful men.]"* (Romans 3:3-4 AMP).

Gentleness. To be gentle is to be humbly submissive. *"Take My yoke upon you and learn from Me, for I am gentle and lowly in heart, and you will find rest for your souls"* (Matthew 11:29).

Self-control. Having control over selfish passions and desires that would pull us away from God. Self-control is needed now more than ever with distractions increasing.

Chapter 4

Dressed for Success

BE DRESSED FOR SUCCESS; DON'T EVER LEAVE HOME OR GO INTO battle without *the armor of God*. Battling spiritually is like participating in football or wrestling where you will need to assume a strong and rigid stance. By maintaining the correct posture, position, and stature, you can withstand the hits and blows of the opposition and not fall. Every piece of God's armor is strategic. We are in God; therefore, His armor fits.

Every day I put on the fullness of God's armor. But before I do, my mind and heart must be right before Him. I ask Him to search me, wash, cleanse, and forgive me. I cannot put clean clothes on over filthy rags, or it will be a stench in the nostrils of God. I encourage you to do the same each day.

The book of Ephesians is where we learn we are spirit beings, our fight is in the spiritual world, and the importance and power of the armor of God:

> *Finally, my brethren, be strong in the Lord and in the power of His might. Put on the whole armor of God, that*

you may be able to stand against the wiles of the devil. For we do not wrestle against flesh and blood, but against principalities, against powers, against the rulers of the darkness of this age, against spiritual hosts of wickedness in the heavenly places. Therefore take up the whole armor of God, that you may be able to withstand in the evil day, and having done all, to stand.

Stand therefore, having girded your waist with truth, having put on the breastplate of righteousness, and having shod your feet with the preparation of the gospel of peace; above all, taking the shield of faith with which you will be able to quench all the fiery darts of the wicked one. And take the helmet of salvation, and the sword of the Spirit, which is the word of God; praying always with all prayer and supplication in the Spirit, being watchful to this end with all perseverance and supplication for all the saints (Ephesians 6:10-18).

I would like to highlight each verse from this passage of Scripture because each is an important focal point regarding God's armor:

Verse 10—*"Finally, my brethren, be strong in the Lord and in the power of His might."*

His might is resurrection power, which came through the sacrifice He made, taking back the keys to death, hell, and the grave.

Verse 11—*"Put on the whole armor of God, that you may be able to stand against the wiles of the devil."* We are in a spiritual battle, but Jesus disarmed the enemy through His death on the cross, making it possible for us to stand firmly and confidently against his schemes.

Verse 12—"*For we do not wrestle against flesh and blood, but against principalities, against powers, against the rulers of darkness of this age, against spiritual hosts of wickedness in heavenly places.*"

Verse 13—"*Therefore take up the whole armor of God, that you may be able to withstand in the evil day, and having done all, to stand.*"

Verse 14—"*Stand therefore, having girded your waist with truth, having put on the breastplate of righteousness.*" It is the belt of truth. He has called us to be holy and with His truth we are binding ourselves to it. There are times when I am attacked by the enemy that I use Scriptures to gird me for whatever is needed at that time. I ask the Father to increase my breastplate every day, to guard and protect my heart for out of it flows the issues of life. When His glory fills my heart, there is no room left for anything else except Him.

Verse 15—"*and having shod your feet with the preparation of the gospel of peace.*" We must have His peace that surpasses all understanding fill our heart and mind so we can take the gospel of peace to others. It needs to be a continual fresh fire of God renewing us. Peace allows us to walk over and through many dangers as we follow it. As I walk in God's peace, His fire burns down the lies and tactics of the enemy and disarms them. God's fire is His Spirit, which goes before me to burn away the chaff, leaving the wheat. As a controlled fire line contains a wild fire, God's holy fire suffocates the enemy's flames of destruction and destroys the works of the enemy. Blessed are the peacemakers for theirs is the Kingdom of God. It is one of the greatest gifts to carry peace in the midst of turmoil. It is amazing to see how peace diffuses the enemy.

Verse 16—"*above all, taking the shield of faith, with which you shall be able to quench all the fiery darts of the wicked one.*" Traditionally, oil was applied to the face of a shield to help deflect arrows. Being anointed by the Lord works in a similar way in our lives. The anointing oil extinguishes arrows, or words, being shot at you.

Verse 17—*"And take the helmet of salvation, and the sword of the Spirit, which is the word of God."* The helmet is given to us to protect and guard our minds. The crown of thorns that Christ wore on His brow was to bring soundness and wholeness of mind. If you are not right in the head, your body will not function properly. Our helmet takes many hits of negative thoughts and doubt each day. The sword is the Word of God. Christ became the Word, and it is His words that we need to cut and penetrate our hearts so that we may speak His words to defeat the enemy. We overcome satan by the blood of the Lamb, and the words of our testimony. Let's grab His word, lining up our lives to what He says.

Verse 18—*"praying always with all prayer and supplication in the Spirit, being watchful to this end with all perseverance and supplication for all the saints."* When you talk to someone with earthly language, the words you are speaking are being broadcast in the natural realm. When you pray in tongues, however, this is a spiritual language that cannot be defined by earth. The words you speak when you pray in the Spirit are being broadcast in the spirit realm, the heavenly places. We are to always be praying in the Holy Spirit who will enable us to persevere, no matter the circumstances we face.

Whatever you are dealing with, grab a Scripture and stand on it! Let His Word penetrate any and every situation you are dealing with. Become the most determined person you have ever met. The verse I stand on is Acts 16:31: *"Believe on the Lord Jesus Christ, and you will be saved, you and your household."* That means me and my children and future grandchildren will be saved and *radically* serve God all the days of our lives! Speaking the word of God is powerful! My mouth is to be a horn that is anointed by God. Saul was anointed from a flask, and David by a horn (1 Samuel 10:1; 1 Samuel

16:13). This anointing will give me great boldness to proclaim His holy name.

In addition to putting on our armor for ourselves, it is important to remember that others are dependent on us. Just as the armor covers us, we must also help cover those around us in love. *"For as the body is one and has many members, but all the members of that one body, being many, are one body, so also is Christ"* (1 Corinthians 12:12). Recognize that while we have been granted the authority to manage our own souls and bodies, with God's help, we are still part of one body—the body of Christ. Our spouse, children, family, job, home, land, church, and ministries are all given to you by the Father, and it is important that we guard what we've been entrusted with.

"When a strong man, fully armed, guards his own house, his possessions are safe. But when someone stronger attacks and overpowers him, he takes away the armor in which the man trusted and divides up his plunder" (Luke 11:21-22 NIV). This is the church!

We have the privilege of serving alongside our brothers and sisters in the faith and playing an important role, no matter what that role is. Being connected with others is like weaving in the fabric of the armor of God—it's what makes us strong. *"But you, beloved, building yourselves up on your most holy faith, praying in the Holy Spirit"* (Jude 1:20). Encourage yourself and stand in faith. Faith will destroy all the lies, fear, and deception; not only from satan, but also from those you love. Build yourself up in your most holy faith for yourself and for them.

Congratulations! You are now dressed for success!

Chapter 5

A Mindset for War

And these signs shall follow them that believe; in my name shall they cast out devils; they shall speak with new tongues; they shall take up serpents; and if they drink any deadly thing, it shall not hurt them; they shall lay hands on the sick, and they shall recover (Mark 16:17-18 KJV).

THERE ARE MANY WEAPONS IN OUR ARSENAL FOR WARFARE. Second Corinthians 10:3-5 speaks about how we must pull down strongholds. A stronghold is a fort, fortified, which must be torn down and removed.

For though we walk in the flesh, we do not war after the flesh: (For the weapons of our warfare are not carnal, but mighty through God to the pulling down of strong holds;) casting down imaginations, and every high thing that exalts itself against the knowledge of God, and bringing into captivity every thought to the obedience of Christ (2 Corinthians 10:3-5 KJV).

The word "carnal" means to be worldly and of the flesh, not of the spirit. To struggle with a carnal mind often means you've received salvation through Christ, but there is a battle raging in your mind between the flesh and the spirit. We are born into this carnal world, and God breathed His Spirit into us. To have victory of the carnal mind, the key is to align your mind with God's Word daily. We must continue to allow ourselves to be washed with the water of God's Word (Ephesians 5:26) in order walk in the Spirit as we are called to do.

WE HAVE ALL AUTHORITY IN JESUS' NAME

Then the seventy returned with joy, saying, "Lord, even the demons are subject to us in Your name." And He said to them, "I saw Satan fall like lightning from heaven. Behold, I give you the authority to trample on serpents and scorpions, and over all the power of the enemy, and nothing shall by any means hurt you. Nevertheless do not rejoice in this, that the spirits are subject to you, but rather rejoice because your names are written in heaven" (Luke 10:17-20).

Is it possible that we have a difficult time believing what the Word says we can do? I did. I thought, *Not me, Lord; I don't have what it takes.* For months I kept reading this passage in Luke over and over. I needed it to become a reality and alive in my heart. I needed to believe I was worthy because of what He had done. God has no favorites, which means that what He will do for one person, He will do for everyone! We were all created equally in the eyes of the Father.

Renewing your mind is a weapon to use to destroy all arguments and obstacles that rise up against what God says. If you've been in a rut, you have become comfortable with lies that are limiting you. I urge you to find Scriptures that specifically address that rut, and verbally declare the truth and promises of God's Word into that circumstance. *No more lies!* Know that the power of Jesus can set you free. There is a promise in James 4:7 that if we submit to God and resist the devil, he must flee! There will be bumps and bruises along the way, and although a bad bruise does hurt, it will heal.

DEFENSIVE AND OFFENSIVE WEAPONS OF PRAYER

Defense: The act or power of defending or guarding against attack, harm or danger; to protect.

Offense: Attitude or position of attack; an attack or hostile action by armed force.

Personally, I won't go into any deliverance situation or do any spiritual mapping—reviewing the spiritual history of a location—without utilizing the defensive and offensive weapons the Lord has given us. It is our job to be ready for any situation that comes our way, in season and out, and these tools help us to be victorious in every situation. Let's look at each tool—faith, speaking in tongues, thanksgiving, agreement, authority, fasting and prayer, praise, and unity—more closely:

Faith—Faith is a complete trust or confidence; a steadfast hope. We must make some exchanges in our weaponry. We have been called to carry the sword of faith, but unfortunately, many of God's people carry the sword of fear, which has ruled too many for too long. My prayer is that you will learn how to unsheathe your sword and release your faith and not be subject to the fear that satan desires you to be trapped in. The Father's desire is that we use our swords not against each other, but rather to make use of the two-edged sword of His Word to disarm lies, cut away fear, break chains of bondage, and bring freedom.

> *"Have faith in God," Jesus answered. "Truly I tell you, if anyone says to this mountain, 'Go, throw yourself into the sea,' and does not doubt in their heart but believes that what they say will happen, it will be done for them. Therefore I tell you, whatever you ask for in prayer, believe that you have received it, and it will be yours"* (Mark 11:22-24 NIV).

Speaking in Tongues—This weapon of prayer allows us to pray in the Spirit with our heavenly language. At times when I'm praying in the Spirit, I feel an unction of the Lord, where a righteous indignation arises in me. When this happens, there is a shift in my prayer language, and I can tell that the things I am declaring in my heavenly language are being directed at the enemy. I refer to this as my warfare tongue.

> *Likewise the Spirit also helps in our weaknesses. For we do not know what we should pray for as we ought, but the Spirit Himself makes intercession for us with groanings which cannot be uttered* (Romans 8:26).

Thanksgiving—Thankfulness dismantles the lies the enemy wants us to believe about our circumstances and glorifies God in the process. *"And we know that all things work together for good to those who love God, to those who are the called according to His purpose"* (Romans 8:28). It might not always feel like tough times are working good in our lives, but even the most difficult circumstances will be forced to line up for our benefit!

Every day I remind myself:

> *Finally, believers, whatever is true, whatever is honorable and worthy of respect, whatever is right and confirmed by God's word, whatever is pure and wholesome, whatever is lovely and brings peace, whatever is admirable and of good repute; if there is any excellence, if there is anything worthy of praise, think continually on these things [center your mind on them, and implant them in your heart]* (Philippians 4:8 AMP).

Agreement—Agreement with the Father's perfect will to be released and agreement with others when contending for breakthrough—both are essential. *"Again, I say to you, that if two of you agree on earth concerning anything that they ask, it will be done for them by My Father in heaven"* (Matthew 18:19).

Authority—Recognizing that Christ's sacrifice has given us authority in both heavenly and earthly places. *"Assuredly, I say to you, whatever you bind on earth will be bound in heaven, and whatever you loose on earth shall be loosed in heaven"* (Matthew 18:18).

Fasting and Prayer—Abstaining from food and activities for the purpose of focusing on God are powerful spiritual disciplines. *"So He said to them, 'This kind can come out by nothing but prayer and fasting'"* (Mark 9:29).

Praise—Giving honor and glory to God, with a heart of admiration. *"They were also to stand every morning to thank and praise the Lord. They were to do the same in the evening"* (1 Chronicles 23:30 NIV). *"May the praise of God be in their mouths and a double-edged sword in their hands"* (Psalm 149:6 NIV).

Unity—God has placed power in our partnership with one another, and being united is a powerful weapon against the enemy's schemes to divide us. There is so much truth in the statement united we stand, divided we fall. *"How good and pleasant it is when God's people live together in unity!"* (Psalm 133:1 NIV).

We must use our weapons of prayer. Use the authority in Matthew 18:18 (NIV) that says, *"whatever you bind on earth will be bound in heaven, and whatever you loose on earth will be loosed in heaven."* Let's get to know Jesus on a deeper level, being changed into His image by the renewing of our minds—to avoid ever hearing *"And the evil spirit answered and said, 'Jesus I know, and Paul I know; but who are you?'"* (Acts 19:15).

The following are some truths I make a point to review, contemplate, and practice each day:

I take communion, to honor. I know that I am the bride awaiting the Lord's return. By remembering His sacrifice, I am strengthened inside as I reflect on what Jesus has done and continues to do for me. I encourage you to read and reflect on 1 Corinthians 11:23-32 and *"The cup of blessing which we bless, is it not the communion of the blood of Christ? The bread which we break, is it not the communion of the body of Christ?"* (1 Corinthians 10:16).

The Lord's Prayer, to seek. He is my Father and I seek His face, help, and will each day. Read and reflect on the Lord's Prayer in Matthew 6:9-15.

Surrender, to submit. I relinquish all control of my life to God to be used for His perfect will. I pray for my spouse, family, and ministries. *"Strangers shall submit themselves unto me: as soon as they hear, they shall be obedient unto me"* (2 Samuel 22:45 KJV).

Releasing of Fire, to protect. I anoint my home, yard, and driveway every day, and release a wall of fire around it all. *"For I, saith the*

Lord, will be unto her a wall of fire round about, and will be the glory in the midst of her" (Zechariah 2:5 KJV).

Needs of others, to deliver and heal. I pray for the needs of others who need prayer. I believe that the Lord is rising again with more strength upon the intercessor, those who petition Him day and night, making needs and requests known to Him. Jesus prayed for His enemies, even those on the crosses next to Him. We must humble ourselves and start lifting up one another. It is all for Jesus! *"You, my brothers and sisters, were called to be free. But do not use your freedom to indulge the flesh; rather, serve one another humbly in love"* (Galatians 5:13 NIV). *"Then I set my face toward the Lord God to make request by prayer and supplications, with fasting, sackcloth, and ashes"* (Daniel 9:3).

I use this analogy often: If you want to be a soul-winner, you have to sow seed. If you want to have a baby, you need the seed to be sown in your womb. If you want the Kingdom of Heaven, you must sow into your prayer time and worship with God. Nothing can effectively and healthily grow strong without spending quality time with the Father. Think back to the parable of the sower from Matthew 13. God can do so much with a soft heart, and nothing softens the heart quite like being in the presence of the Father.

RESIST THE DEVIL

"Therefore submit to God. Resist the devil and he will flee from you" (James 4:7). One of the greatest offensive weapons the Father has given us is to resist the devil. There are going to be times when you may feel battered and bruised; but after a while, the devil will realize that there is no door open for him to come through, and he will flee…leaving you alone.

I went through horrendous torment and fear for years of my adult life; I could not sleep, eat, or even think clearly. However, the stronger I became in God through His Word and prayer, the less frequent the devil's attacks came. When you resist the devil, he will flee; it is a promise in the Word of God.

Our mindset is very important. If you don't know who you are in Christ Jesus and the rights you have as a child of the King, you will not have victory. People who don't know their God-given identity often possess a defeatist mindset. Therefore, a daily renewing of your mind must take place, and that begins by reclaiming the helmet of salvation to cover your mind! Through the benefits of putting on your spiritual armor daily, piece by piece, you are also able to come into a place of rising above situations and circumstances.

Being equipped with the armor of God allows you to hold on to a vision—your spiritual sight. The Word says that people without a vision perish (see Proverbs 29:18). When we continue to ignore the spirit world and the need for offensive and defensive actions, we lose our spiritual sight, our vision. Remember, there are graveyards full of visions and dreams, and ministries that died, never being fulfilled. How tragic and sad, because one seed is all it takes to produce a forest! Remember, Jesus said, *"…if you have faith as small as a mustard seed, you can say to this mountain, 'Move from here to there,' and it will move. Nothing will be impossible for you"* (Matthew 17:20 NIV).

Once your armor is intact, learning who your enemy is and how to defeat him every time is a strategy that must be implemented into your everyday life. Many people have said, "We shouldn't focus on the enemy. We just need to focus on God." That is how the enemy uses a lying spirit to get you off of his back! Hosea 4:6 states, *"My people are destroyed for lack of knowledge."*

There has never been a king, ruler, or general who has not intently studied his enemy to know his patterns, tactics, weaknesses, and strengths. That is how wars are won, kingdoms are taken, and dominions overthrown! The foundation of their victories lies in *knowing who they are*. This is combined with a confidence to hold their position and stand in the knowledge of why they are defeating this enemy.

My desire is to help the church have a clearer understanding that God is real, but so is satan. Knowing your enemies is where we begin. We wrestle against principalities, powers, rulers of darkness of this world, and spiritual wickedness in high places. The opposing forces of this world are very strong, but the light of Jesus overcomes all powers and opposition. Do not forget—the devil belongs under our foot. He may bruise our heel, but that's it.

> *He has delivered us from the power of darkness and conveyed us into the kingdom of the Son of His love* (Colossians 1:13).

> *Then the seventy returned with joy, saying, "Lord, even the demons are subject to us in Your name* (Luke 10:17).

We are fighting against the enemy on many levels. We are contending for a soul to receive salvation, Christ, and redemption from sin—to become a new creation through Christ's sacrifice. We are fighting through intercession for others and for restoration from sickness and family problems. When dealing with deliverance and exorcism from strongholds and demonic possession, it is vital we know God's plan and our level of involvement. On battlegrounds of this nature, you must seek and hear from the Father on how involved you should be. *Never* go to battle unless Jesus calls you to, especially when it comes to this! As I've always said, "Don't go play on satan's playground unless you are called to!" We fight against injustice and we fight for righteousness, but not all battle strategies are the same.

Never in biblical history did anyone lose a battle that God called him or her to fight when they followed His plan. They only lost when they jumped out ahead of God and were overcome with fear, pride, or greed. If you are called to do battle, there is a process that I have found to be effective in my fight:

- Receive a clear understanding from the Lord.

- Identify what you are fighting against—self, spirits, demons, etc.

- Research history. Map out a history of roots in the family tree, city, state, or where the need is, also known as spiritual mapping. For example, you can't have lasting victory over a weed in your garden if you don't pluck it at the root, because in another season it will come back, releasing others. Begin warring over these strongholds.

- Pray for discernment for the situation, family, etc.

- Ask the Lord for a battle plan. How is He specifically calling *you* to do it? Strategy is the key. Lay aside all preconceived ideas you have. Get before the Father and pray, petition, and fast, and He will show you how to complete the task.

The people who walked in darkness have seen a great light; those who dwelt in the land of the shadow of death, upon them a light has shined. You have multiplied the nation and increased its joy; they rejoice before You according to the joy of harvest, as men rejoice when they divide the spoil. For You have broken the yoke of his burden and the staff of his shoulder, the rod of his oppressor, as in the day of Midian. For every warrior's sandal from the noisy battle, and garments rolled in blood, will be used for burning and fuel of fire. For unto us a Child is born, unto us a Son is given; and the government will be upon His shoulder. And His name will be called Wonderful, Counselor, Mighty God, Everlasting Father, Prince of Peace. Of the increase of His government and peace there will be no end, upon the throne of David and over His kingdom, to order it and establish it with judgment and justice from that time forward, even forever. The zeal of the Lord of hosts will perform this (Isaiah 9:2-7).

The following are some key truths the Father gives us in this passage in Isaiah 9. You can no longer walk in darkness, because Jesus is your light and He has consumed the death. The Lord has enlarged our nation and increased our joy, just like if we had walked into the enemy's camp and taken back all of our possessions. He has shattered and broken off our yokes that have burdened us, but also has broken the oppressor's rod, so he can no longer use it against us. You cannot go into any battle without removing garments from the last battle. Remove those bloody garments; verse 5 is a very important key. As we walk in His zeal, He will robe us in the garments that represent His nature; some examples are Prince of Peace, Mighty God, Counselor.

PRAYER

Father, right now we demolish every satanic assignment that has been held in the second heaven against our lives. We thank You right now that You are dis-enthroning every assignment. Thank You, Lord, for Your revelation, and that You have created (insert your name) to be a force that cannot be reckoned with! Activate to accelerate!

These are not the days of Elijah. Why? Because we are the Elijahs of our day. Signs, wonders, and miracles flow through me and this reader, Lord. Bless us with wisdom to do the impossible and the gift of faith, Lord, to do the miraculous. We believe, Lord, in Your name, Jesus. May radical faith right now rise up in every situation of our lives. May heavenly, angelic encounters release the captives. We position ourselves for Kingdom alignment and advancement. I declare that destiny favors this dear reader this very day. Amen.

Chapter 6

SATANIC EVILS

Many people are confused about the purpose and prevalence of satanism in our world today. Even many Christians seem unaware of the fact that there is widespread and organized occult activity in every nation on earth. People wonder if it is real, and if so, what shape does it take? Society has changed so much over recent decades, with many cultures sharing ideas and practices with one another, which means satanism has taken on many new forms. While some are obvious, others are harder to detect. The majority of people who dabble with satanic practices or beliefs do not realize what they are partnering with; they unwittingly fall under the control of the prince of the power of the air.

> *Wherein in time past ye walked according to the course of this world, according to the **prince of the power of the air,** the spirit that now worketh in the children of disobedience"* (Ephesians 2:2 KJV).

People are largely ignorant about this prince and have been led astray by the undertones of darkness that permeate our culture.

However, there is another group of people who know exactly what they are doing and still rush headlong into darkness. They engage in exactly the kinds of rites and practices, willfully partnering with the demonic in exchange for power. Sadly, knowing full well what they are doing, the ramifications it has, and still pursue darkness headlong. In either case, neither are accessing power through the cross. Accessing power, wisdom, and guidance outside of the cross is witchcraft. Therefore, if they are not serving God, they are serving satan.

> *Do you not know that to whom you present yourselves slaves to obey, you are that one's slaves whom you obey, whether of sin leading to death, or of obedience leading to righteousness?* (Romans 6:16)

We can choose to respond correctly and not be conformed to the world. The promise being that we can know His will for our lives. Just as Paul writes in Ephesians 4:26-27, *"Be angry and do not sin: do not let not the sun go down on your wrath, nor give place to the devil."* Be angry but don't sin. There is a difference between reacting and responding to a situation. To *react* is typically quick, without much thought, and can be tense and aggressive. To *respond* is more thought out, calm, and nonthreatening. It is important that even if our anger feels justified, we take time to pause and ensure we are responding to the situation, thus avoiding the potential for sin to abound in that moment. It is hard to not react in anger or frustration. We can apply being a living sacrifice in Romans 12:1-2 (NIV):

> *Therefore, I urge you, brothers and sisters, in view of God's mercy, to offer your bodies as a living sacrifice, holy and pleasing to God—this is your true and proper worship. Do not conform to the pattern of this world, but*

be transformed by the renewing of your mind. Then you
will be able to test and approve what God's will is—his
good, pleasing and perfect will.

Before starting your journey through the pages of this chapter, I would like to reflect on some of the changes that have taken place in the past twenty years since I first sat down and started writing a journal. I had to understand what was going on and how to deal with what was happening. The things I felt the Father revealed to me in visions or knowledge thirty years or more ago—whether in part or whole—have been coming to light.

When I saw visions of demonic activities becoming commonplace and even accepted within society, I couldn't believe it. But here we are three decades later, seeing darkness show itself in plain sight all over the place. Every three months there is an equinox or solstice when witches are out in public places throughout the United States. I now live in Washington State, where it is like Disneyland for the demons, blown wide open, and witches come out every three months like clockwork.

I believe people have become more embracing of the dark arts, so to speak, because they are looking for authenticity, power, answers, acceptance, love; you name it, they want it. And satan is all too eager to grant their desires, or at least a very realistic looking façade of their desires. But we are the church and we are to stand up against the darkness. We have every weapon in our arsenal to defeat him.

Credit: © DailMail.com
By Emily Crane and Ash Tulett and Chris Spargo For Dailymail.com
Published: 17:15 AEDT, 25 February 2017

New York witches are out in the open, in front of Trump Tower. They are on news shows demonstrating how to cast spells, especially against President Trump and the government. They are openly releasing curses involving the president and cabinet members. Crowds are drawn to them as they watch. Many are recruiting the weaker links in society—street kids, runaways, misfits, homeless, curious—anyone who feels abandoned or not wanted by others or society. Like a fly lured into a spider's web, witches make many promises that some believe are true, but are actually words to seduce the hurt and rejected. They promise power and acceptance, whatever their broken hearts desire.

When people are accepted into their world of witchcraft, most cannot get out without help. That's where we the church come in. This is when real ministry takes place, helping people escape from the web the enemy has woven to keep them bound and hopeless. If we as Christians stand up in prayer against the lies and curses, the plans of the enemy will not succeed—we have all authority to demolish the strongholds and spiderwebs in our cities.

I recognize that the nature of work that God has called me to is unique; I do things that most believers would never do, nor should they do unless God has called, ordained, and given them insight. But all believers are called to pray and stand beside one another, no matter what the Lord has called us to do. Everyone is vital.

THE WITCHES' BALL

A few years ago, I traveled out of state to the witches' ball. People from all over the world come once a year to learn and glean from one another. It's what we would call a satanic revival. I remember telling the Lord someone needs to do something! It seems every time I say that, He asks, "Well, what about you?" I prayed, fasted, and really sought the Lord, and then I got up and went. I remember as I was driving close by, hordes of darkness in the spirit were everywhere! It was gut-wrenching and almost had me doubled over. I knew I wasn't just playing with what I call members of the "poser club," people trying to be something they're not. As I walked in the door and looked around, I saw tables set up selling potions, hexes, spells. They also offered training on how to go deeper into the dark arts.

I saw a woman who is very high up in satan's army. Many children sat around her. She did not need to turn to see me because the demons alerted her of my presence by staring and hissing at me. I stood nearby and listened as she spoke to the children. There was a young boy alongside her named Johnny. She was demonstrating her psychic power, using him as an example. Johnny was facing the far wall as she asked him what she was holding in her hand. (Holy Spirit was speaking to me during her lesson, and told me it was a blue stone.) Johnny answered that it was a stone. The demons continue staring at me, hissing even louder than before.

Then she asked the boy what kind of stone it was (as Holy Spirit whispers to me, "Johnny is in My hand"). Johnny told her a blue stone. She pressed him to describe the blue stone, and Johnny answered turquoise. My eyes almost popped out of my head as the demon on her shoulder began talking to another demon, giving insight to the boy! She asked if he knew what kind of stone it was, and Johnny replied a Kingman turquoise with gold running through it. The crowd was astonished, thinking she was demonstrating her psychic powers—but she was in fact listening to demons talking to one another.

I looked over lovingly at Frank, one of the angels I've had with me for as long as I can remember, and I could feel his wings covering me, protecting me. I wanted to go say something to the woman, but Holy Spirit told me not to. I could feel a pulling in my spirit to leave, so I went back out the door. I was so upset! I asked the Father, "Why did You take me in there? You know I will go shut that down!" Then I heard Him very clearly whisper in my spirit, "Your job is to go ahead of the rest and assess the land; to assess what's going on and gather intel. Now go and pray, telling My people what you've seen."

That day still upsets me because satan and his cohorts were everywhere! Parents are raising up their children in the occult and it's normal to them! That is why the information and message in these books and teachings are so important. It says in the Word to train up children in the way they should go and they will not depart (Proverbs 22:6). Yet so many children in Christian families are being fed into this occultist system! I know personally in several public schools they are training up children in dark arts disguised as other things. From satanic after-school programs in Washington State, to promoting required reading like Harry Potter. It is out in the open and now the real battle has begun!

Thankfully, on the other hand, there are children all around the world, little powerhouses I call them, filled with the fire of Holy Spirit who are moving Heaven on earth. They are standing up and fighting back. Perhaps not the kind of fighting back you may think, as children have even greater faith. Childlike faith is powerful!

I have gone to many psychic fairs. While filming for our ministry in Seattle, I went to Pike Place Market. There is a psychic there with a lot of darkness. As I was about to knock, she placed the Closed sign on the door while closing the lace curtains. I said aloud, "You're not closed. I'm standing right here." Then for the first time ever, I said, "Hey, want to play!?" I had to catch myself for a minute—I couldn't believe I said that! The fire that hit me was that of Jehu, Elijah, and Paul. I had to confront these lies. I thought, *Why not me and why not now!* I wondered if she didn't want me to come in because she knew I was going to disrupt the spirit realm, causing her business to shut down. Or maybe the demons knew that if I went in she would be presented with Jesus in a different way.

I walked away with my anointing oil on my hand, and I touched the ground in front of the doorway. I asked God that everyone who considered walking in there would turn around in confusion and walk away. I remind myself all of the time, and I want to remind you, that we are meant to be transformers—we are more than meets the eye! We have so many weapons within our reach to cause mass destruction to the powers of darkness!

Over the past two decades in particular, society's focus has shifted, and it is definitely in the wrong direction. From witches' balls to witches over caldrons openly doing incantations and spells in the streets celebrating their "religion," to media emphasizing the allure and power of magic, to movies about witchcraft drawing millions of children into their grasp and opening the door to so much wickedness and violence—our culture is moving toward darkness and away from God's light. More young children are exposed to sex, drugs, and murder in the media now than ever.

You know you've hit what I call the "OMG" moment when movies teach our children that if they go into a fantasy land of hopes, all of their dreams will come true. They are learning things like, "You have the power to curse someone to death, or have them fall in love with you," and they are drawn to it. I urge you to go to your local library or your children's school library and see how many books on the occult are right at your children's fingertips every day. Make it your business and become aware.

MEDIA INFLUENCE

Stories that emerge from a culture reflect its values and motives; this is why historians study myths and legends in order to understand the heart of ancient peoples. Our present culture is no different, with TV and movies becoming ever more influential and integral to our society. It is apparent that our culture has a massive appetite for the supernatural, and Hollywood has been meeting that need instead of the church.

Two TV shows I have found to be particularly dangerous are *Midnight Texas* on NBC and a Netflix series called *13 Reasons Why*. I feel these shows heavily emphasize darkness and sin and the results that come from agreeing with lies of the enemy. The Father showed me that through television programs like these, the veil between the natural and supernatural is opened—like manhole covers blowing off, allowing an entry point to hell.

Something important to be aware of is that what originates in the spiritual often manifests itself in the physical. A few years ago, I was in Texas preaching for Pastor Pam Neely. The town sits on a thin veil between the living (natural) and the dead (supernatural), a spiritual fault line or ley line. This spot is a dimensional intersection between the two worlds—our world and theirs.

While preaching, I was struck with a flash vision. I felt a paradigm shift hit beneath the ground under our feet. I saw a great body of water, like a damn breaking open. The water came up to my waistline, and I saw Texas was torrentially flooded. A powerful quaking hit my spirit, and I began to receive a word of knowledge. The word was that the flood would come quicker than we realize. A couple days after I left Texas, a physical flood occurred, and the heavy rains came.

I share this to encourage you that when we have an encounter in the spirit, it is always important to be courageous and speak what we see or hear, if we feel prompted to do so. Many people might anticipate receiving a warning from the Father, and everyone is blessed when God provides time for preparation. The church I was speaking at in Texas suffered no damage even though the surrounding area was hit hard. They recognized the word of the Lord and prayed.

I feel the veil between the spiritual realm and the natural has slowly begun to tear, leaving a chasm wide open, and we are watching as it happens. This chasm is like a gateway, and both good and bad can emerge through this gateway. The flood in Texas happened in the natural because in the spiritual the area was being flooded by the demonic and its influence. But take heart! God's mighty warriors will come together as one to stand against the darkness!

The television show *Midnight Texas* showcases psychics, witches, vampires, a serial killer, etc. While we have been created by God to desire connection with the supernatural—Heaven, the angelic, spiritual gifts, etc.—so many churches have stopped teaching about the spirit realm altogether. Hollywood recognizes the hunger people have for the supernatural and has responded by filling the need. But instead of the emphasis being on the wonders of God, it is focused on the powers of darkness. As the church, we can rise up and demonstrate God's supernatural power. Power that comes not at a detriment to us or the lives around us, but power from the cross that brings true freedom, healing, guidance, and wisdom.

The season two preview of *Midnight Texas* showcased a witch from season one with the cliffhanger of wondering if she is a witch of light or darkness. No matter whether they reveal her to be of light or darkness, both types of witches are demonic and very dangerous. There is no such thing as a "good witch," they are two sides of the same coin and receive their power outside of God. It is a tragedy that many people are satisfied going to a created thing as a source of wisdom or power when we have the ability to go straight to the Creator!

The show refers to the town of Midnight as a safe haven for people who are different. So many people, especially youth, feel like they do not belong. If the church isn't known for providing a safe environment for people to come and feel a sense of belonging, the demonic world is all too eager to offer a safe haven from feelings of loneliness and powerlessness—and the offer is hungrily received.

In the late 1990s, the television show *Charmed* opened the eyes of a younger generation to a lighter side of witchcraft. The audience target was early teenagers to millennials. The premise was three witch sisters using their abilities to fight evil to get "the bad guy," but in reality, they were reopening the concept of using magic for personal gain. Their book of secrets contained all their incantations and potions, whatever was needed to cast their spells. Whenever they started to invoke curses, they would open a portal, one dimension into another, to create what I call a demonic jet stream.

We see a similar strategy used in the *Harry Potter* book and movie series, which gained in popularity shortly after the television show *Charmed* aired. Harry Potter opened a brand-new door into the dark arts, and children desperately wanted to become wizards and sorcerers or sorceresses. Most amusement parks in the United States are saturated with wizard or witch paraphernalia. Some even offer classes to become a wizard yourself, learning to cast spells with your own personal wand. The mystery has really "enchanted," a type of spell, a generation into embracing darkness, something our society considered taboo just a couple decades ago. I'm personally so grateful to the creators of *The Lord of the Rings* and *The Chronicles of Narnia* for giving children the ability to go on an adventure paved with goodness and virtues—not an adventure into a dangerous portal like *Charmed* and *Harry Potter*, which only give an illusion of good when its core is based on darkness.

Television programs and movies based on witchcraft and darkness have gained in popularity in the past few years. Another example is *Lucifer* on Fox, based on the original fallen angel in the Bible. The television version becomes dissatisfied with his life in hell. After abandoning his throne and retiring to Los Angeles, Lucifer indulges himself in women, wine, and music. He owns an upscale night club where a murder takes place, which is where he meets a homicide detective, and they begin to solve crimes together. As the TV shows continues, Lucifer starts to wonder if there is hope for his soul. Viewers can see very clearly the manipulation and twisting occurring in this show, but then again that's precisely what the real Lucifer (aka the devil) has done since he was cast down and out of Heaven. He is a shape-shifter, and will transform into whatever is necessary, or whatever it takes to lure you in. In the television show, Lucifer looks like redemption and hope and possibilities, which we know is *not* reality. Darkness is not light.

In my book *Satanism: The Truth Behind the Veil,* I explain that through lust and power, emissaries against God's children are hitting harder than we can even imagine. Images bombard our minds every day. There is really no exact number, but negative images are powerful, and people tend to vividly remember negative images they've seen. Have you ever thought about how a commercial that wants you to buy their product works? The goal of even a one-minute commercial is to inundate you with so much imagery and information that it makes you believe you have to have the product they're selling. Many people are left believing that everything they saw and heard in the commercial is true, and that they can lose weight doing a 3-day juice cleanse (or whatever the commercial's intention is), so long as the person buys into the product being sold.

The same principal applies to our younger generation. The rate of information they are absorbing at an impressionable age is astounding. Satan knows that young minds are developing and learning and stringing together data at a faster rate than any other time in their lives. As they go to school, darkness and corruption are accessible and looking to sway them.

A Great Deception

I believe a great deception has come through many television shows, movies, and video games. Through the sights and sounds display, they lure people in, leaving an imprint, and the thread of deception weaves a tapestry for ultimate destruction. Satan is in no hurry; he is calculated, very cunning, and deceptive. Our eyes are the windows to the world in front of us. Parents and people in general need to stand against what our loved ones receive through their eyes and ears. Who will be a voice for the generations to come? Will it be you? There is a generation of adolescents and teens who need us like never before!

The plot of the television show *13 Reasons Why* on NBC is the story of a girl in high school who commits suicide and leaves tapes of why she did it, as if it were a treasure hunt. As the show opens, a statement on-screen tells viewers where to get help if they or someone they know shows signs or has thoughts about suicide. While I am grateful that they have a reference to the suicide hotline, the show essentially glamorizes suicide. Suicide rate statics since airing this show have risen!

A Colorado school district pulled the novel *13 Reasons Why* from library shelves after seven students committed suicide. New Zealand banned the novel for depicting suicide and sexual violence. Do not allow your children and teens to read or watch this! I agree with those who have made a stand against allowing their community to be affected by this novel. Proper discussion is needed now more than ever about suicide—the glamorization of it portrayed in *13 Reasons Why* is not okay.

I make it a point to know worldwide suicide statistics. Because young men and boys are more susceptible to suicidal thoughts and actions than girls, I see a correlation from the times of Moses and Jesus. The kings wanted to kill the male bloodline of the Jewish people; all babies two years and younger were to be murdered. Now, when dealing with suicide, the demonic power is no different. Satan wants to steal our inheritance—our children are our inheritance! Satan has always been after the male seed, and the rates of suicide are increasing and alarming. We, the body of Christ, must be on alert; the devil seeks to devour and destroy. I know without a doubt that Jesus is our only hope.

Media has an ability to influence young people—to make it seem that what they are watching or listening to is normal. By allowing detrimental movies, music, books, TV, and videos they are opening a door with the potential for extremely endangering consequences. The belief that the occult means acceptance and power and that suicide is a release from pain is dead wrong. These beliefs only bring more destruction. Our eyes really are the windows to our soul. We must help our children safeguard their eye gates as they are forming beliefs about what is healthy.

Such media and shows are the public face of the satanic agenda being imposed on this generation. While adults are definitely swept up and taken in by the darkness, the primary focus is, and has likely always been, on children. If the enemy can get his hooks into youngsters in their formative years, he can send them further and further off of the track that their heavenly Father laid for them when He knit them together. These TV shows are dangerous because of how accepted and even applauded they are. However, the far more obvious threat to family, trust, health, intimacy, and proper communication lies with us as adults.

In this book you will see a theme emerge regarding media, TV, movies, books, music, and the list goes on. We have generations of lost, twisted, and confused people in the world. Many attend church and youth groups, but most of their time is spent with kids from school—who are not raised with Jesus in their homes. Our young people are hit hard enough with just growing up. And the pressures this younger generation deals with all the time wears them down and can lead to destruction. Compromise is not hard to submit to when you want to fit in and have friends.

I have encountered many cases with junior high and high school Christians who dabble in the occult, perform séances, use Ouija boards, and summon demons. Yet the next day they go to church, put their other personality mask on, and behave as their alter ego. There are too many that match this behavior to count.

ON TV IN 2018

Netflix made the announcement that it is adding Kiddy Pornography to the already popular cartoon Big mouth.

The TV show *Anne of Green Gables* will introduce the LGBTQ (lesbian, gay, bisexual, transgender, questioning) to their network (CBC). At one time the series was pure and wholesome; the foundation and message was based on the Bible and God-fearing people.

There is a book titled *Two Santa Clauses*—the two men are married homosexuals. No Mrs. Claus.

Good Morning, America interviewed a young boy dressed flamboyantly with makeup, appearing as a drag queen, on the ABC network.

These are just a few of the hundreds of unacceptable and corrupting shows on networks now or coming soon. We have a serious identity crisis in all areas in all the world, causing chaos and turmoil that blows in winds of confusion.

Where is our indignation? Where is the church? Have we become so desensitized that we have abandoned our moral obligation to uphold the standards of Christ? If so, we will sadly see pastors, priests, and Christians fall to the ways of the world and indecent behavior.

In the school systems of America, and throughout the world, the United Nations' radical agenda pushes LGBTQ education where it is becoming mandatory in preschool and upward grades. Parents seem to have no voice regarding what their children are being taught or instructed. Matthew 24:12 (NIV) decrees, *"Because of the increase of wickedness, the love of most will grow cold."* I am trying to wrap my mind around the insanity that is behind allowing kindergarten children to be taught about boy and girl anatomy, transgender, and the LGBTQ movement. In many nations girls in their early teens are having mastectomies and other physically altering operations in order to become the opposite sex.

We must be voices like John the Baptist. The vacuum of not standing up for truth and justice has had such a rippling effect. We can reverse this curse and fight back. God's Word says:

> *If My people who are called by My name will humble themselves, and pray and seek My face, and turn from their wicked ways, then will I hear from heaven, and will forgive their sin and heal their land* (2 Chronicles 7:14).

> *My people, who are called by My Name, humble themselves, and pray and seek (crave, require as a necessity) My face and turn from their wicked ways, then I will hear [them] from heaven, and forgive their sin and heal their land* (2 Chronicles 7:14 AMP).

I pray Heaven's miracle to come upon the earth in full force. Awaken Your people, Lord. May we repent for the compromise and not understanding Your ways. I ask that You will help me to trust in You with all my heart, to not lean on my own understanding, in all my ways acknowledge You, and You will direct my footsteps. The key here is my understanding, for it is so limited. Lord, forgive me. Help me to stand where I have fallen or compromised You, including others, and have a bold witness of the gospel. In Jesus' name, amen.

PORNOGRAPHY

It is generally understood that many men, and a rapidly increasing number of women, with computer access, view pornography on a regular basis. It is pervasive. Advertisements with material that was once considered soft porn are being used in commercials and many public places. Unbelievably provocative images and jokes or references to certain kinds of sex acts are unrestricted as well. With the constant use of this warped projection of sexuality, children are getting exposed to, and becoming curious about, sex at a very young age. If a young child is unsupervised on the Internet, it is quite unlikely his introduction to sex will be the "birds and bees" talk from his parents.

As young as 9-year-olds are exposed to pornography. Many become addicted to it at this early age and are bound by the perverseness. Nine years of age. All it takes for a curious boy or girl to access pornography of the vilest sort is a simple Internet search away. The size of this problem and the effect it has on our culture is impossible to understate, and yet it is still not seen as a problem to be addressed by everybody who can make an impact.

There seems to be a large portion of society that have no problem with letting their children be educated about sex by a predatory industry that thrives on violence and degradation, one that frankly has nothing to do with sex but everything to do with the immediate gratification of lust. Have we fallen so deeply down the immoral rabbit hole that our cities can be compared to Sodom and Gomorrah? Have we become desensitized to our culture of addiction?

Sexual sin is especially dangerous because of the crushing and debilitating shame that comes with it. The shame runs so deep because of the lack of honest and open discussion about it. Unfortunately, it seems that the hindrance to a transparent conversation is the fact that many are drawn in to it one way or other. Statistics indicate very little difference in the prevalence of pornography addiction in the church compared to the rest of society. This is alarming!

Matthew 5:13 (NIV) says that the church—we believers are to be the salt of the earth: *"You are the salt of the earth. But if the salt loses its saltiness, how can it be made salty again? It is no longer good for anything, except to be thrown out and trampled underfoot."* We must sit down with children and have real conversations about sex and the importance of abstaining from sex until marriage. God created sex to be a special act of joining together between a husband and wife.

If some of the church is compromised in this area, then how can we stand up and lift our voices for truth and sexual integrity? First Peter 4:17 warns, *"For the time has come for judgment to begin at the house of God; and if it begins with us first, what will be the end of those who do not obey the gospel of God?"* It is time for us as a family of believers to really confront and own this issue. There will be literal hell to pay if we do not. We will lose spouses, alienate our children and parents, and worst of all alienate ourselves from the call of God on our lives.

We can take responsibility and do everything we can to solve it. We have the keys necessary to set people free from not only drugs and alcohol, but also sexual addictions. It is deeply entwined with self-worth and false intimacy, and satan uses this to cause isolation. Remember that we are never alone. The Holy Spirit is always ready to help set us free!

> *By the humility and gentleness of Christ, I appeal to you—I, Paul, who am "timid" when face to face with you, but "bold" toward you when away! I beg you that when I come I may not have to be as bold as I expect to be toward some people who think that we live by the standards of this world. For though we live in the world, we do not wage war as the world does.* ***The weapons we fight with are not the weapons of the world. On the contrary, they have divine power to demolish strongholds.*** *We*

demolish arguments and every pretension that sets itself up against the knowledge of God, and we take captive every thought to make it obedient to Christ. And we will be ready to punish every act of disobedience, once your obedience is complete (2 Corinthians 10:1-6 NIV).

I love how the King James Version of 2 Corinthians 10:5-6 says, "*Casting down imaginations, and every high thing that exalteth itself against the knowledge of God, and bringing into captivity every thought to the obedience of Christ. **And having in a readiness to revenge all disobedience, when your obedience is fulfilled.***" Our flesh has to come under submission to God. It's difficult to effectively wage war against the enemy when you are fighting a battle within yourself. If you struggle with any form of hidden sexual sin, please understand that there is hope and help for you.

Our Father is gracious and compassionate and will never leave you, He does not see you as damaged goods. There is a process of restoration that He is just yearning to set in motion, but it may be that you need to take the first step. Find somebody you trust, likely of the same gender as yourself, and let the person know what you have been struggling with. This may be uncomfortable, but the temporary discomfort of owning up to your problems is absolutely nothing compared to suffering with an addiction that will eat away at your conscience and may devour relationships, time, money, and cost you your walk with God. Once sin is out in the open, the devil and his cohorts can't bully you anymore or add shame and fear. Amen to that!

FOLSOM STREET FAIR

Every September in San Francisco, California, and Berlin, Germany, there is a Folsom Street Fair. This is a "bondage, discipline, dominance and submission, sadomasochism" (BDSM) fetish event. It is totally demonic and dark, teeming with perversion and lust. The season starts in July with a few selected parties, ramping up to the one event in September. In San Francisco it spans over thirteen city blocks and has more than 400,000 attendees annually. What started out in the 1970s as a small event has morphed into a massive swelling of public sex, whippings, and many other things I will omit. Many businesses struggle this weekend, as customers avoid the area due to the public sexual acts with the event participants getting out of control. Most folks are wearing only harnesses or nothing at all.

I attend the Folsom Street Fair in San Francisco yearly, having trained teams to share the love of God with not only the attendees, but the coordinators. We go to demonstrate His love, bring healing, prophecy, and His greater presence into the darkness. They know I am a Christian and just want to love the people. The release of the book *50 Shades of Grey* has brought an increase in curious people coming to explore what BDSM is all about. In 2016, I was joined with a team to film and document what I do.

The first two years I attended, we set up tents where people could come and I would prophesy over them. They would wait in line for hours for a "Free Reading." Tears fell freely from the shock of a word of knowledge, and the Christian love they felt. Most were prodigals, many came back to Christ, and all were touched by our heavenly Father. In year three, I was asked not to bring tents. You see, something was happening, an army was rising up, we were changing the atmosphere!

For the filming, Janelle Wilson, a dear friend of mine, was part of the team to help with the interviews. The event is darkness, through and through. In one of the interviews a young man was asked, "Do you ever feel suicidal? If so, did you wake up wanting to kill yourself today?" After this word of knowledge, he said to me as he was fixing his makeup, "Yes, yes I did!" The demon that was on him literally turned around and stared right back at me. I, in turn, prayed, bound up that demonic spirit and blessed him. I would have done a full-blown deliverance right there in the restaurant, but I followed the Lord's instruction. Suicide is the second leading cause of death, suicide!

Many in the LGBTQ community are hopeless and helpless. They are so confused. The demons within cause confusion regarding a sense of identity. Many are outcasts, no one wants them, not even their parents. That is why every year this and many other events of this type are growing in numbers. Those attending and involved need to find a place to belong and express themselves. Yearly I interact with hundreds to thousands of people at fairs, street evangelism, strip bars, etc. I recently put together a half-hour program dealing with the LGBTQ community. My hope is to awaken the church to begin to love these people, rather than push them down and away. We must remember the Scripture: *"Therefore, I tell you, her many sins have been forgiven—as her great loved has shown. But whoever has forgiven little loves little"* (Luke 7:47 NIV).

LESBIAN-GAY-BISEXUAL-TRANSGENDER-QUESTIONING (LGBTQ)

*Therefore I urge you to reaffirm your love to him. For to this end I also wrote, that I might put you to the test, whether you are obedient in all things. Now **whom you forgive anything, I also forgive.** For if indeed I have forgiven anything, I have forgiven that one for your sakes in the presence of Christ, lest Satan should take advantage of us; for we are not ignorant of his devices* (2 Corinthians 2:8-11).

In the world today, we have an epidemic on our hands. We have a generation that struggles with gender identity—they are so confused and lost. No one should ever feel as if they cannot be comfortable in society, and especially within their own skin. Many believe they didn't get the specific genes for the gender they were born with. There is a huge worldwide culture that revolves around embracing the LGBTQ community. Numerous times I've spoken to people who have said, "I should have been a girl, but was born a boy." I worked in the sex industry before I was saved, so I have an understanding of how lies and truth-twisting can erode someone's self-image. The lies cause many to think they should appear differently, believing they need to have a complete sex change.

Because of the work I have done over several years, I was invited to San Francisco by a prayer team from California. They asked me to come and train, equip, and help demonstrate God's love at a public sex fair. As I prayed, in like a blink of an eye, I said, "I see no Light there."

They reassured me, "Oh yes, there is."

I said, "NO, there's not. Are there any churches, booths, tents, or teams out witnessing truth?"

They said, "There is one."

To confirm, I went to the event website, and BAM, there it was. A sign over a booth read: "Christian and Gay is OK." My blood pressure rose up. I said, "This is not God, this is the devil!"

They replied, "The booth is letting them know Jesus loves them."

He does love them. I grabbed my Bible and made this statement as I slammed it on the table, "I have a Holy Bible. Now I don't know what kind of Bible you have, but apparently it's not God's word. Nowhere does it say that being gay and married to the same sex is okay."

They were upset and offended by my remark. I was not out to offend them. I explained my purpose for the discussion, "If I'm going to lead a team to war and battle, training under the mantel of AGM (Angela Greenig Ministries), then it will be done in holiness. If you do it the way God's blueprint is played out, then we will have a great victory." They listened.

While it is important that we as the church reach out and embrace people who are bound, we cannot condone the behavior. The church struggles so much with the LGBTQ community. In the same way we would reach out in love for someone struggling with self-mutilation, we can demonstrate His love and the power that we carry to set people free. This bondage is so entrenched in the psyche of a person, often beginning at a very early age, it could take a lot of time for deliverance and healing. Helping someone who is stuck in this lifestyle is not only about removing the spiritual bondages, but allowing God to bring a reworking of thought processes and self-image while we reach out to and support people God is working on, embracing them. Please hear me, and see the difference.

Youth bound by unclean spirits for years and cutting themselves would be supported and encouraged to see their self-worth. But we would never give them a knife and encourage them to keep cutting themselves! Churches have watered down the gospel to become seeker friendly; let's just call it what it is, in one word, compromise! There is a great cost to compromise. By compromising and not helping others to walk in the joy of freedom, but to allow them to remain bound and believe that is okay! The bottom line, God's Word decrees from Leviticus 20:13 *"If a man lies with a male as he lies with a woman, both of them have committed an abomination."* Remember that we are not here to judge, but to encourage, coach, and demonstrate the love of God.

In 2018 I was invited to a drag queens' ball. While there, people were drawn to me and many of the queens and gays came up to me and asked why I was there. I told them, "I'm a pastor, I love Jesus, and I love you too." Two out of three commented that if I had a church in that area, they would come. I looked puzzled at them. One of the most well-known queens in the world said to me, "Angela, maybe God brought you here to be a bridge builder." BAM, I could have been raptured right then! I just got up out of the boat and walked on water.

My prayers are that I can start raising up people in cities worldwide who will go and preach the Good News of Jesus Christ. Preach the Good News without judgment and in His love. The greatest tragedy I see and deal with is people feeling segregated and feeling all alone. I knew all too well that feeling of rejection and hurt. And I know that because I came out of the hell I lived in, so can they. It was not, and still is not, complicated. The plan is blueprinted in His Holy Word, the Bible.

Advice for all the moms, dads, and families who have had their loved ones taken away or changed by this lifestyle: The enemy's deception has them brainwashed (like satanism), believing that they were called to be a different sex, or are gay. Whatever the case may be, you are to keep praying and stand your ground. Find those who are on fire and filled with the power of the Holy Spirt. There will be tough days in this battle, but find a support system that can be an Aaron to you, lifting up your arms in the battle. Some, like me, are out there preaching, praying, and sharing the love of Jesus. You are not alone. Jesus hears your heart and prayers. We can and will win this war one soul at a time. You will see in the teaching that there are three spirits operating—lying, seducing, and perverse spirits. Jesus overcomes them all.

SATANIC AFTER-SCHOOL CLUB

While preparing for the Folsom Fair a few years ago, I received several calls asking me to come and pray with groups in Seattle against a satanic program. I told them I was not able to at the time. As the conversation continued, I urged one group to go and take action themselves, so they did. The action they took was on their knees in prayer, holding candles. I explained later that this was a powerful approach, as they were making their voices heard their own way. I told them, "You're trimming back the branches to bring exposure, amen, and that's so important, but next time rip that flippin' tree right out of the ground!" We must take our places now.

In Mark 11:12-25, Jesus sees a fig tree not bearing fruit, curses it, and it withered and died from the roots up. Although many branches on a tree may still be able to bear fruit, it does not mean the tree is thriving, or that it will continue to bear fruit. While prayer is powerful and can shift things, in the Folsom Fair situation I felt that prayer was like trimming spiritual branches instead of removing the source of power. My thought is to tear the tree out completely—roots and all. I believe we are in a time and place right now where we must draw that line in the sand, and we have a decision to make—we either follow through all the way until the job is completed, or we don't go at all.

If darkness does not have any light illuminating a pathway for salvation to come to the lost, then how will those trapped in the darkness find the way out? God's Word is called a lamp unto our feet, a light unto our path (Psalm 119:105). Where there is no Word, there is no light. Where there is no Word, there is no hope, which brings separation from God. He created us specifically to be with Him. There are so many people hungry and desperate for a touch from God, and to see light overcome the darkness. We are meant to be light-bearers, but they will not see unless we go. It is time to stand up for truth and justice and dispel darkness with His glorious, transforming light!

The following is an article from the *Christian Post* written by Michael Gryboski and published on August 1, 2016, titled "Satanic Temple Launches 'After School Satan Club' in Attempt to Counter Christian Groups":

A group called The Satanic Temple has founded and launched a nationwide after-school club to counter Christian student organizations in public schools.

Known as the "After School Satan Club," the group's creation comes in response to the Christian Good News Club that meets at public schools throughout the nation.

Douglas Mesner, spokesperson and co-founder of The Satanic Temple who goes by the name Lucien Greaves, told The Christian Post that the Christian clubs being at public schools "created the need for a counter-balance in the extracurricular options."

Graves claimed that "While the Good News Clubs teach children shame, guilt, and fear —that they will die and be tormented in Hell—the After-School Satan Clubs will focus on art projects and education with no religious opinion inserted. The program is merely created and operated by The Satanic Temple. There is no attempt to indoctrinate the children."

Greaves told CP that nine schools have already set up satanic chapters, and he expects that increased media attention has led more students to express an interest in starting their own clubs. "We've received a flood of volunteer inquiries from people wanting to establish our program in schools that host the Good News Clubs near them," continued Greaves. "Many of these prospective volunteers claim certification in teaching, some of them are grandparents, and all are very supportive of what we're doing."

The Good News Club is a ministry of the nondenominational group Child Evangelism Fellowship and boasts over 4,500 chapters nationwide. In 2001, the United States Supreme Court ruled 6-3 in the decision Good News Club v. Milford Central School that the Christian group had the right to meet on public school property after school hours.

"By denying the club access to the school's limited public forum on the ground that the club was religious in nature, Milford discriminated against the club because of its religious viewpoint in violation of the Free Speech Clause," wrote Justice Clarence Thomas for the majority. He continued, "…it cannot be said that the danger that children would misperceive the endorsement of religion is any greater than the danger that they would perceive hostility toward the religious viewpoint if the club were excluded from the public forum."

Moises Esteves, vice president of USA Ministries for Child Evangelism Fellowship, told CP that he believed the Satan club was "yet another atheist PR stunt" that "has no staying power. The 'After School Satan Club' is simply another attention-seeking atheist club. The choice of mascot reveals that its leaders simply hate God, and are trying to provoke or spook parents and schools," said Esteves. "Like those before it, this club will fizzle out, because parents don't view their children as pawns for a 'blend of political activism, religious critique and performance art' by angry atheists."

Esteves of CEF added that he believed that ultimately the GNCs will outlast the Satan clubs, because "at the end of the day, parents know what is best for their children. When children are already struggling with many issues like violence, drugs, physical bullying and online bullying, gangs, etc., the last thing that parents want for their children is a Satan Club," continued Esteves. "Good News Clubs have encountered similar clubs before, and parents overwhelmingly choose the GNC. Beyond some flyers or one or two meetings at most, 'After School Satan' clubs will not have any impact."

While he's opposed to the mission of the satanic club, Esteves told CP that if it "doesn't do anything illegal, they have the same legal rights as anyone else" to meet at schools.[1]

The billboard shown in the photograph is just one of many created by The Satanic Temple to promote the after-school satan club. Can you imagine your children having easier access to darkness than this?

Another advertisement inferred that if your child is being bullied, the club can teach them how to cast spells. The desire of parents is to make sure their child feels safe, and when faced with a hopeless situation, parents can become desperate for a solution to help their child. These billboards were strategically designed to provide parents and children with just that—a "solution" to the problems they face: bullying, unpopularity, loneliness, rejection, etc. (Photo Source: www.kuow.org.).

When we, as hopeless parents or concerned believers, drive by these billboards on our way to work, school, church, anywhere at all, we realize that they catch the attention of struggling children and parents alike in their satanic net of deception and empty promises. I believe a major shift in the spiritual atmosphere and the physical environment has occurred since this program launched. God gives us signs all the time, but sadly we have grown accustomed to seeing the signs and often become visually impaired and unable to see what He has highlighted for us to combat.

SOMETHING BIG

I knew something big was coming again. Perhaps not quite to the magnitude of what happened in the United States on 9/11, but I knew I was on the wall, and this watchman "wasn't going to play." On April 16, 2017, Resurrection Sunday, the country of Turkey had a radical shift in their government. The new president in office wanted to dissolve the parliament and convert the nation to Islam.

I believe that Turkey has been the "number one gate" for demonic activity for many years. In the Bible, the city of Ephesus— located in modern-day Turkey—was not only the first church, but it was also home to the goddess Diana, or Artemis, where pagan worship ran rampant (see Acts 19:23-41).

During a conference I held in San Francisco in November 2011, the word was out that the Mayans and New Age believers collectively came together to hold strategic meetings. By January 1, 2012, these groups began taking their thirteen crystal skulls across America.[2] Their tour began in New York—the first passageway for immigrants entering the United States—then throughout North America. Their intent was to release sounds that would bring "harmony" to America and blessings to the earth and to the people, brought through the reuniting of the thirteen crystal skulls.

From December 10 through 12, 2012, I rented a bar in San Francisco on Mission Street, known as one of the darkest and most violent areas. What an incredible time we had evangelizing and feeding the homeless. We invaded the city for the King!

On 12/12/12, 120 of us "suited up" in our worship and took communion, then headed out to pray and prophesy on the Golden Gate Bridge and over the cities, decreeing blessings against the curses. It was a sight to be seen, as the Jewish flag was being waived, two shofars blew before us, and we began our procession across the bridge. Many people were marching as one body with one common purpose.

There really are no words to describe what was happening on the bridge that day. We even discovered later from a friend of mine in Israel that at precisely the same time as we were crossing the Golden Gate Bridge, a ministry was at the Golden Gate in Israel, also blowing shofars and decreeing a sound that would resound around the world. The Lord was uniting his people across continents for His glory! It is just so profound and incredible to me how He does that.

On the third and final evening of our rally in San Francisco, as we decreed, warred, and worshipped, at 11:11 p.m. on 12/12/12, every time the enemy released his sound, so did we. I had purchased a Mayan signet ring many months prior leading up to the event, and at the climactic moment of the evening, at 11:50 p.m., my husband, Larry, took a rock and crushed the ring until it was flat, to symbolically represent our authority to crush the head of our enemies with one swift wield of our sword.

With every blow of the shofar and every praise lifted to Heaven, the sound ROARED louder and louder all across the land. We were establishing a branch of the Reformation Army, arising in response to the clarion call of our Lord. In the Spirit I saw a blue flame ignite all around us. As you take a closer look in the picture, you can see a sword piercing through the crowd. Pure light! I knew it was finished.

The very next day, the morning of December 13, an earthquake shook from San Francisco to the Mayan pyramids and ruins where they worshipped. The earthquake registered a 6.3 on the Richter scale. According to my study of spiritual significance in numbers, the number 63 represents Israel.

Come on, you just can't make this stuff up! What an incredible time we had! Honestly it was a hard war! I believe every time we take that leap of faith, God not only meets us, but this is what builds up our faith for the next time. Many times you will need to encourage yourself. David, being the shepherd boy, was trained to protect the sheep. Only the bravest and strongest men were able to kill a lion (Judges 14:5-6)—and David did. When it came to confronting Goliath, David knew he could. Why was he preparing all his life for such a time? It wasn't about the bear or the lion, he was preparing for Goliath. He didn't have to second-guess himself. He had a confidence that only happens through trials, failures, and victory. Can you imagine if David had said, "Well, I don't have what it takes. I'm nobody. I can't fight against the giant." He could have looked to his older brothers and thought, *They are men, they're trained. They have armor. They got this!* Sound familiar? It should, because we react many times to where we are right now, not to our potential.

Our potential is where God can use us the greatest. We see are our failures, but God sees our potential; just as He sees the victory, so can we. He sees the lion and the bear defeated. This is our time to stand on the shoulders of giants and carry off their heads from the battlefields. Whatever that giant may be, we take Goliath's head off and all other giants that defy the army of God!

PROTECTING OUR FAMILIES

You may still be wondering what else you can do to protect your children and loved ones from this darkness. As parents and loving believers, we have the right and a need to know what is happening in and around children's lives! Become aware of how children are using technology, what books they are reading, what music they are listening to, and what social media they are using. Make it your business.

You may think, *Geez, Ang...!,* but even cartoons like *Sponge Bob* have satanic symbols. When our children were growing up, we did not allow them to watch *The Simpsons.* Many said, "It's not a bad show," but it has some more-than-suggestive content. Even, or more so, with teens, pay attention to what they watch and do on their cell phones. Monitor what they're surfing on the Internet and block any sites, shows, or games that have a rating you do not approve of. Check their rooms. Parents have every right to oversee each area of their children's lives.

When our daughter was in kindergarten, I visited the school principal the day before school started. I asked to see the library and was shocked at what I saw. Thirty-something years ago they had zero Bibles—yet there were many occult and ghost stories books. I was glad I looked. The next day when she started kindergarten, there were two brand-new kid's Bibles that we donated to the library. Shortly after school began, I signed up to work with Child Evangelism Fellowship (CEF). I taught two groups of children each week in my home until my children were in high school.

COMMUNICATE!

Communicate is perhaps the most important advice I can give. Set the tone for respectful conversation—listen to what children and teens are saying and speak life into them. Open communication is the greatest way to safeguard your family. Proverbs 6:2 (NIV) says, *"You have been trapped by what you said, ensnared by the words of your mouth."* The meaning of ensnare is to be trapped. I refuse to be trapped! We will always have things come into our minds, but until they are spoken, then and only then will they bring life or destruction. Remember to think before you speak and to keep your words loving, but firm, that you mean business.

Stand firm in your faith and convictions without compromise! If by chance things are already in the house, then you have all authority to take care of business. Luke 11:21 says, *"When a strong man, fully armed, guards his own palace* [home], *his goods are in peace"* There may be a battle, and a majority of the time it will get worse, but stand your ground and be strong.

Guidance Prayer: Father in Heaven, we ask for the families and the parents out who perhaps are not seeing the signs, or are not sure what to do for their loved ones caught in the lust and perversion of the world, shine Your light and bring conviction and purity to their hearts and minds. Help them see the rebellion of what they're doing to themselves and their family. I pray, Holy Spirit, don't let them turn to the left or the right, but let true repentance and healing begin. In Jesus' name, amen.

The few stories that I have shared are to reveal one thing—I am just a donkey Jesus rides in on; no one special, just a daughter of the King. I say sometimes, "Devil, you should have killed me while you had the chance." Remember, God is God, and satan is not! The realm of the demonic kingdom is very complex, but we have to be educated, remembering that the Bible says, *"My people are destroyed for lack of knowledge..."* (Hosea 4:6 NIV).

The only reason I began writing was honestly to help myself understand my God-given rights and authority. From the experiences of many great aches and pains is why I do what I do to help train your hands for battle by teaching and training seminars, to give you the tools needed to defeat the enemy. More importantly, to open your eyes from the impossible to become the possible, and know that together we can do this.

As we go deeper now into the Sixteen Demonic Strongholds, you may think, *Oh my gosh, that's me, and that's why I can't seem to be free! I take two steps forward and five steps back.* I believe with you, in the name of Jesus, His breaker anointing will not only set you free, but help you help others as well.

These are the keys that the Lord gave me to defeat the enemy. It is Christ's redemptive, finished work at the cross. The blood, His word, His love, and His Holy Spirit will destroy all of the lies and entrapments of the enemy.

ENDNOTES

1. https://www.christianpost.com/news/satanic-temple
    -launches-after-school-satan-club-in-schools-nationwide-to
    -counter-christian-groups.html; accessed February 4, 2019.

2. The legend of the thirteen crystal skulls is that in a pivotal
    time in human history, the skulls will be reunited to awaken
    a new era—transforming an old paradigm into a new world.
    These skulls are believed to be between 5,000 and 35,000
    years old and archaeologists were told by locals that the
    skulls possessed magical powers and healing properties.
    For more information: https://worldtruth.tv/the-13-crystal
    -skulls-mystery-2/; accessed February 5, 2019.

Chapter 7

SATANISM

THE FRUITS OF SATANISM ARE OFTEN MASKED AND SUBDUED. THEY are underlying and subversive. This reflects the nature of satan, the original imitator, illusionist, and deceiver.

> *Do you not know that to whom you present yourselves slaves to obey, you are that one's slaves whom you obey, whether of sin leading to death, or of obedience leading to righteousness?* (Romans 6:16)

> *Now is the judgment of this world: now shall the **prince of this world** be cast out* (John 12:31 KJV).

> *Wherein in time past ye walked according to the course of this world, according to the **prince of the power of the air**, the spirit that now worketh in the children of disobedience* (Ephesians 2:2 KJV).

GOD CREATED LUCIFER— THERE IS NO EQUALITY

A few years ago, I participated in Darren Wilson's film *Furious Love*. It was to expose the devil, the occult, and how to help people get out of the darkness. I was and am known by this statement, "God is God and satan is not." The devil will always want you to look in the side or rearview mirror to keep looking back. But remember, things "may appear larger than they really are." God wants us to see through the windshield. It's big. It allows you to focus on life's journey; as you keep looking ahead, you will see correctly.

> *How you are fallen from heaven, O Lucifer, son of the morning! How you are cut down to the ground, you who weakened the nations!* (Isaiah 14:12)

The word "Satan" in Hebrew means the accuser or adversary. He was a great angel created perfect and good. He was appointed to be a minister at the throne of God, yet before the world began, he rebelled and became the chief antagonist of God and humanity. In his rebellion against God, satan and a multitude of angels, we identify after their fall as demons or evil spirits, were thrown out of Heaven. Satan caused the fall of the human race when Adam and Eve gave in to deception.

Satan's kingdom is a highly organized empire of evil that has authority over the kingdom of the air. Satan is a shape shifter; he can come to you in the form of beauty or like in my dream, taking the form of a child. Satan is not omnipresent, omnipotent, or omniscient; therefore, most of his activity is delegated to his demons.

Jesus came to earth to destroy the works of satan, establish God's Kingdom, and deliver us from satan's dominion by His death and resurrection. Christ initiated the defeat of satan and we are assured of God's ultimate victory over him. Satan's goals are to kill, steal, and destroy. Some weapons in his arsenal that he uses are to lure, distract, and intimidate. Believers must pray and be alert concerning his schemes and temptations, and resist him: *"Be alert and of sober mind. Your enemy the devil prowls around like a roaring lion looking for someone to devour"* (1 Peter 5:8 NIV).

> *The thief does not come except to steal, and to kill, and to destroy. I* [Jesus] *have come that they may have life, and that they may have it more abundantly* (John 10:10).

The word "destroy" in this context means to utterly abolish. The Word tells us that the devil is out to kill us, steal from us, and destroy us. He will plant seeds of suspicion in your *mind*, try to weaken your *will*, and will play with your *emotions* to try and steal your soul. The devil will do whatever it takes to assassinate and highjack your destiny. He will inflict pain and sickness to your body and try to weaken your spirit. Remember, the devil hates you, because he knows how fearfully and wonderfully God made you, and how powerful you are.

But our focus must not be on the devil or his so-called "power," rather our focus must be on the Father and His *"exceedingly great and precious promises"* (2 Peter 1:4). Pray about the choices you make so they will produce life—stand strong in the faith that God has given you. He is a good Father and will not allow you to be tempted more than you can bear (1 Corinthians 10:13). God will always provide a means of escape so you can rise victoriously above your circumstances. Remember, FAITH is spelled R-I-S-K. Don't allow fear to dictate your faith.

In Ezekiel 28, God speaks about satan—before his fall from Heaven:

You were in Eden, the garden of God; every precious stone adorned you: carnelian, chrysolite and emerald, topaz, onyx and jasper, lapis lazuli, turquoise and beryl.

Your settings and mountings were made of gold; on the day you were created they were prepared. You were anointed as a guardian cherub, for so I ordained you. You were on the holy mount of God; you walked among the fiery stones. **You were blameless** *in your ways from the day you were created* **till wickedness was found in you** (Ezekiel 28:13-15 NIV).

I believe that from the time of the Garden of Eden until today, satan has been targeting our five senses. Satan comes as a snake in the garden, or even as an angel of light. He speaks and intends to draw you into his dark world. I've always found it interesting how satan shape-shifted into a snake and peddled his snake oil through that forked tongue. James 1:14-15 (NIV) says, *"But each person is tempted when they are dragged away by their own evil desire and enticed. Then, after desire has conceived, it gives birth to sin; and sin, when it is full-grown, gives birth to death."* We may be in this world, but we must refuse to be part of it. Our negative thoughts must be taken captive. On average experts estimate that between 60,000-80,000 thoughts a day run through our minds. That's an average of 2,500-3,300 thoughts per hour!

Satan knows the power of envy all too well. He is a rebellious, jealous, coveting liar. His objective is draw humankind to want more; to be equal to or above another person or God Himself. He wants God's position. In Numbers 16, the spirit of Korah tells the same story. He gathered a few hundred men of great standing and position in the community and led a rebellion against God's chosen leader, Moses. The story ends with the ground opening up and swallowing the men and their families. Many died that day because of Korah's covetousness.

> *Now the serpent was more cunning than any beast of the field which the Lord God had made. And he said to the woman, "Has God indeed said, 'You shall not eat of every tree of the garden'?" And the woman said to the serpent, "We may eat the fruit of the trees of the garden; but of the fruit of the tree which is in the midst of the garden, God has said, 'You shall not eat it, nor shall you touch it, lest you die.'" Then the serpent said to the woman, "You will not surely die. For God knows that in the day you eat of it your eyes will be opened, and you will be like God, knowing good and evil." So when **the woman saw** that the tree was good for food, that **it was pleasant to the eyes**, and a tree desirable to make one wise, she **took of its fruit and ate**. She also gave to her husband with her, and **he ate.** Then the eyes of both of them were opened, and they knew that they were naked; and they sewed fig leaves together and made themselves coverings. And **they heard** the sound of the Lord God walking in the garden in the cool of the day, and Adam and his wife hid themselves from the presence of the Lord God among the trees of the garden* (Genesis 3:1-8).

Our five human senses are the key in this Scripture passage: sight, touch, smell, taste, and hearing.

1. She saw the tree—*sight.*

2. She took of the fruit—*touch.*

3. Although not mentioned, I believe she could *smell* the aroma of the fruit.

4. She did eat—*taste.*

5. They *heard* the voice of the Lord.

> *Then the Lord God called to Adam and said to him, "Where are you?" So he said, "I heard Your voice in the garden, and I was afraid because I was naked; and I hid myself." And He said, "Who told you that you were naked? Have you eaten from the tree of which I commanded you that you should not eat?"* (Genesis 3:9-11)

There was a perfect order in creation. All was amazing until satan seduced Eve with the fruit. He twisted the words of God just enough that she doubted and then took and ate and her eyes where opened. What was once peace and order in the world was now chaotic for Eve and Adam. When order is absent, chaos enters in.

This act of disobedience brought forth death in the lives of Adam and Eve—and to every generation afterward. Since then, two systems of government have been in operation—God's and satan's. Now we have the carnal nature and the spiritual nature at work within us and within the world.

To understand satan's schemes, it is important to understand the specific strongholds and spirits that he uses to deceive you and me. We are about to go into depth about the sixteen demonic strongholds; but before we do, let's pause for a moment to take a deeper look at what sin is. Sin are the acts we commit that are contrary to God's will; sin is the evil power or nature that causes us to commit the sin. Sins are also known as transgressions.

Transgression (trans-gresh'-un): From "transgress," to pass over or beyond; to overpass, as any rule prescribed as the limit of duty; to break or violate, as a law, civil or moral; the act of transgressing; the violation of a law or known principle of rectitude; breach of command; offense; crime; sin.

In the Old Testament, the word *pesha`* occurs eighty times, rendered in all versions by "transgression." Its meaning is rebellion. The word "rebellion" differs from this word in that it may be in the heart, though no opportunity should be granted for its manifestation: *"An evil man seeks only rebellion"* (Proverbs 17:11). Here the evil man, or person, contemplates an evil heart, looking for an excuse or opportunity to rebel.

The New Testament uses the Greek word parabasis, "trespass": *"The law...was added because of transgressions"* (Galatians 3:19). *"Where there is no law there is no transgression"* (Romans 4:15). *"For the redemption of the transgressions under the first covenant"* (Hebrews 9:15).

Transgression is also defined as iniquity, sin; wickedness; evil: *"Set a guard over my mouth, Lord; keep watch over the door of my lips. Do not let my heart be drawn to what is evil so that I take part in wicked deeds along with those who are evildoers; do not let me eat their delicacies"* (Psalm 141:3-4 NIV).

We must deal with iniquity and transgressions in our lives. They can be inherited from our mother or father's bloodline (nature), or things we've been taught or experienced (nurture). Regardless how they've entered, we must face the battle within and align ourselves with God's Word to overcome them. The five senses made me think, *Lord, is that why we walk by faith and not by sight? Trusting in your Holy Spirit?*

PRAYER

Father, we boldly come before Your throne room right now, and we lay all—state your sins and burdens—before the altar. I thank You that we can boldly come to You, and stand in faith; our banner is truth and justice through Christ's blood. Lord, we make a conscious decision to raise up our children in the way they should go, using Your Word and discipline. I pray right now for such an awakening of parents and families that are raising up this next genera-tion. I am asking that our children become game changers and revival makers; that governments would be changed by these young lions and lionesses. Lord, they have a godly destiny and a high call.

I pray, Father, that we would be living sacrifices and examples as we walk by faith and not by sight. I pray and plead Your blood, Jesus, and I ask You to wash our youth. Forgive us for allowing the media to shape our children. I pray, Lord, that You will give wisdom and revelation to schoolteachers, youth pastors, and leaders on how to impart and train our children, please. Thank You, Lord, right now that we are going to rescue the younger generation who are attending psychic classes and after-school satanic programs, learning how to curse and send incantations to get what they want. God, You are God and satan is not. It's time we take back every generation in Jesus' powerful name, amen and amen.

IMPORTANT KNOWLEDGE AND DEFINITIONS

Occult

The word "occult" means to conceal or hide; to go far beyond human understanding. It includes mysticism, black magic, astrol-ogy, and divination. It is the force that is often used and considered innocent to the unaware. This often includes Christians who may place trust and belief in mediums to answer their questions instead of consulting their all-knowing God.

So you are aware, the commercials on late-night television touting psychic hotlines aren't reading your future, they are typically listening to demons that speak to them. They then tell you all about yourself, and consequently you open doors that give satan access to come in whenever he wants; to release his entrapments. We, just like King Saul, must not open doors that God has told us not to.

> *Now the practices of the sinful nature are clearly evident: they are sexual immorality, impurity, sensuality (total irresponsibility, lack of self-control), idolatry, sorcery, hostility, strife, jealousy, fits of anger, disputes, dissensions, factions [that promote heresies], envy, drunkenness, riotous behavior, and other things like these. I warn you beforehand, just as I did previously, that those who practice such things will not inherit the kingdom of God* (Galatians 5:19-21 AMP).

The Sigil of Baphomet (see graphic) is the formal symbol of the Church of Satan. It dates back to the Knights Templar. The pentagram—the upside-down 5-sided star—also called the pent alpha, is associated with the releasing of demons. It is also called the endless knot and has either a goat or ram's head within two circles. It means "the hidden ones" or "he who abides in all things." The Egyptian Neter Amon, when talking about the pentagram, said that dark forces can move and change things in the natural, pulling them into the supernatural. Within the two circles is written (in Hebrew) the word "Leviathan." It is read from the bottom up, on the right side and counterclockwise.

You will notice that there are many different pentagram symbols. Various cults use various versions, depending upon their beliefs. Here are just a few cults that use the symbol: Pythagoreans, Masons, Gnostics, Cabalists, magicians, Wiccans, and Satanists.

The names "Samael" and "Lilith" are inscribed in the pentagram. The marriage of these two is known as the "Angel Satan" or the "Other God." These two beings are believed to have birthed a demonic race. Many scholars argue that Lilith was Adam's first wife. Samael (Samael or Iblis) is also called the adversary, the Prince of the World, the Prince of the Power of the Air, the Poison Angel, Chief of the Satan's, Prince of Demons, Magician, the great serpent with twelve wings that draws after him, and the Angel of Death. Lilith is also called Bat Zuge, the Enemy of Infants, the bride of Samael, and the Angel of Prostitution.

> *Then God said, "Let Us make man in Our image, according to Our likeness; let them have dominion over the fish of the sea, over the birds of the air, and over the cattle, over all the earth and over every creeping thing that creeps on the earth." So God created man in His own*

image; in the image of God He created him; male and female He created them (Genesis 1:26-27).

Cult

A "cult" is a particular ritual or system of worship; an extreme devotion to one's belief. By mere definition of the word, Christianity could be considered this as well, but only regarding having an extreme devotion to our belief in God. Beyond that, the "system" of worship becomes man (or FLESH) made, and is no longer of the Spirit of God. Although cults may vary in what is worshipped and how their beliefs are exercised, *they do not represent Christianity.* Therefore, if they are not of God, they are serving satan.

Psychic Realm

The psychic realm invades our soul—mind, will, and emotions. This is the area where mediums and witches infiltrate the mind of people with curses, spells, incantations, etc. It is a dark spiritual world, a "one world order" with satan as their master. Deuteronomy 29:29 says, *"The secret things belong to the Lord our God, but those things which are revealed belong to us and to our children forever, that we may do all the words of this law."* Psychics can call and summon up familiar spirits that do their work for satan. Just as the prophet prays and the Holy Spirit will speak to him or her, the psychic will conjure up a familiar spirit.

Remember that satan attempts to imitate and falsify anything that is real and of God. There will be times when you will feel mentally disconnected, all of a sudden you're in the middle of a sentence and you can't remember and feel confused. Whenever I start getting really hit hard, when I'm going into a deliverance or into a city, whatever it is the Father's calling me to go and do, when I start to get hit like this, I know I have witchcraft curses coming against me. I remind myself, *Ange, it's psychic curses coming in to hinder you.* At times, even before I get there, I can see the place, the layout of the room, cities, and nations where I am going. It has taken more than thirty-five years to learn how to navigate through this, and I always pray this prayer: "Father, in the name of Christ Jesus, I bind every word spoken against me and I put a hedge of thorns around them."

The battle is real, I encourage you to repent and give your heart to Jesus—or satan will drag your soul to hell. Your choice, you choose. I've always stood on the promises in Isaiah 58:1-12, and pray you do the same. We have been called to loose the bands of wickedness, free the oppressed, care for the poor, rebuild the ancient ruins, and see restoration of all God created. Let's bring the lost home. I want all those in the occult, as many as I can reach to know the love of Christ Jesus.

Many people suffer as victims of circumstances, whether from childhood, teen years, or adulthood. When someone has been raped or abused, it is the start of behavioral problems resulting from developing harmful thought patterns. Our brains store collected data from all our negative experiences, which keeps us in bondage.

Matthew 13 speaks clearly of the wheat and tares. The tares are sown unexpectedly in our lives and they open when we least expect them. Just like the tares, the psychic realm will invade these areas of our mind to twist and pervert them against us. It will dredge up places and things in our past in an attempt to bring them back into our conscious mind and have us dwell on them.

God has called us to walk by faith and not by sight. The familiar spirit will have you see through the lens of the carnal eye—but God calls us to walk by sight like in Genesis 3. Adam and Eve walked every day with God until they sinned. Can you imagine seeing the Father every day and the scope of your lens was 20/20? That means you saw the angels and the spiritual realm. We are called to be the seers and knowers of our times.

*Brothers and sisters, I do not consider that I have made
it my own yet; but one thing I do: forgetting what lies
behind and reaching forward to what lies ahead, I
press on toward the goal to win the [heavenly] prize of
the upward call of God in Christ Jesus. All of us who
are mature [pursuing spiritual perfection] should have
this attitude. And if in any respect you have a different attitude, that too God will make clear to you.
Only let us stay true to what we have already attained*
(Philippians 3:13-16 AMP).

The psychic world is very complex and seducing, and we've only
really scratched the surface of it here. I cover this subject more
in-depth in my book, *Demons & Angels*, breaking down the hierarchy of the demons and of the angelic. My book, *Satanism: The
Truth Behind the Veil*, offers deeper understanding specifically on
satan himself as the deceiver of believers and how he operates.

Generational Curse

Just as we have physical traits that link us to our families (brown
eyes, blonde hair, etc.), we can also have mentalities and spiritual-
ties in common with our ancestors. Our genes carry our physical
attributes, and our spirits likewise can be the result of what has
been imparted to us from our ancestors. These can be generational
blessings or possibly curses. We obviously need to continue to build
on the blessings to be passed on to our future generations. In the
other realm, we need to break the curses that have been transferred
over the bloodlines of our families. If not, it could be that curses
increase in our bloodline instead of blessings.

*You shall not bow down to them nor serve them. For I, the
Lord your God, am a jealous God, visiting the iniquity*

of the fathers upon the children to the third and fourth generations of those who hate Me (Deuteronomy 5:9).

We can cancel out sickness, cycles of abuse, whatever it may be, by decreeing this day no more. Sever the ungodly soulish ties to family curses. Refuse to have any more diseases that lead to death or keep you bound to poverty, barely getting by. Stand strong and stand your ground.

> *Another parable He put forth to them, saying: "The kingdom of heaven is like a man who sowed good seed in his field; but while men slept, his enemy came and sowed tares among the wheat and went his way. But when the grain had sprouted and produced a crop, then the tares also appeared"* (Matthew 13:24-26).

Often what is started with good intentions has bad results. This is what becomes of the lives of God's intended people, whether it be of their own experience or what has been continued from their parents and their parents before them. Whether it is incest, alcoholism, or whatever the iniquity is that has been handed down, it is usually done in secret and shame. The victims live in darkness and fear, thinking that their behavior is their fault, or that what was done to them (rape, abuse, etc.) is their fault. They believe that if they had only done something differently, their lives would be better. Just as the weeds are sown prior to birth and throughout our lives, our lives contain the good and the bad. Being germinated by traumas, disappointments, and deaths, they mature and choke us as the tares. However, just as the wheat, God can open His goodness and expose the badness so it can be seen and destroyed.

PRAYER

Job 22:28 says, "You will also declare [decree] a thing and it will be established for you; so light will shine on your ways."

I decree that God's light is shining brightly and illuminating your way!

I decree that whatever place in the spirit realm that has been broken in to is secure and the enemy is bound from operating there.

I decree that the glory of the Lord has risen upon you and that you can discern the territory that God has given to you.

I decree that there is light everywhere you place your feet.

I decree that your devotion time is filled with the glory light of God. The Lord is your everlasting light (Isaiah 60:19).

I decree Ephesians 1:18 (NIV), that the eyes of your heart may be enlightened so you may know the hope to which He has called you.

I decree First Peter 2:9, that you are of a chosen generation, a royal priesthood, a holy nation, His own special child, that you will proclaim the excellence of Him who called you out of darkness into His marvelous light.

I decree that others will come out of darkness into His marvelous light as you proclaim His praise. And, out of their gloom the eyes of the blind shall see (Isaiah 29:18).

Lord, You are light and You annihilate the darkness. You shine brightly in and through us (Psalm 18). Thank You,

Lord, the light of the knowledge of the glory of God that will be released through for the advancement of Your Kingdom and the fulfillment of Your promises!

Lord, shine bright so we can see Your light!

DELIVERANCE—POSSESSION OR DEMONIZED?

I believe that years of working to help people be set free from being possessed or demonized is not enough. It needs to be known what is inhabiting, or affecting, a being. There is a difference. Demon possession attacks the soul—mind, will, and emotions—and can cause physical and personality changes. Often people become animalistic as they change, showing more primitive behaviors and sounds—growling, snarling, slithering, etc.

In the case of a child or adolescent, most parents will see changes in their clothing choices and the way they react. I want to make this very, very clear—when dealing with adolescent teenagers, many are simply trying to figure out who they are. They are looking to what society considers acceptable via magazines and the media to understand what is considered cool, dope, hip, etc. Some do want to serve satan, but most are unaware of what they are getting involved in, particularly regarding music, psychic hotlines, Ouija boards, tarot cards, and New Age beliefs. Many times young people are hurting, lost, and need love. They are seeking what God has readily made available to them, but they don't see it because they are blinded by the darkness.

For Christians, it is typically a case of being demonized rather than possessed. I call it a "hit and run" attack. Unfortunately, they do not see it, yet hope whatever it is will go away. It's temporary, but can be terrorizing. It stays awhile, long enough to shake you up, and then goes away for a time. It does not take possession, but can inflict serious damage. It can be any given spirit: anger, fear, jealousy, etc.

The point is, with the help of this book, it is my sincere prayer that you will learn not only who you are in Jesus, but you will know how to use God's weapons of warfare. It is the same as when you learned to drive a car. Initially you were cautious, not being confident in what you were doing, but then you studied, practiced, gained confidence, and earned your license. This is essentially the same way you will earn your place in God's army, as long as you are led by the Lord to go and face the enemy.

There is power in numbers. In the beginning of my learning about spiritual warfare, which is a continual journey, I would ask a friend to pray and agree with me, then I would proceed to bind up the spirit, cast it out in Jesus' name, and curse the fruit of the strongman. We then would pray for healing, loose the fruit of the Holy Spirit, and anoint to seal it with the oil of joy. It is important, once we lead a person to the Lord, to have them filled with the Holy Spirit immediately. This will fill in the gaps and holes from the darkness that was in their spirit with the light of Christ.

Jesus demonstrated the importance of numbers as well. In both Mark 6 and Luke 10, the Bible speaks of how Jesus sent the men out two by two. In Matthew 18:20, the Lord says, *"Where two or three are gathered together in My name, I am there in the midst of them,"* and Deuteronomy 32:30 says that one can chase a thousand and two can put ten thousand to flight. Sometimes you will not feel or see with your eyes that a deliverance has been accomplished, but do not box God in to what you can perceive; you will see it by the fruit in that person afterward. Remember, the Word says, *"According to your faith let it be to you"* (Matthew 9:29) and *"For we walk by faith, not by sight"* (2 Corinthians 5:7). Yes, you can ask God to give you faith to believe, and you will receive!

All I know is that I never go and play on satan's playground unless God calls me. Know that even when I go and do according to plan, there have been counterattacks. What are they, you ask? We see the antics of the enemy in situations such as when the car won't start, the phone has static at the most important moments of a conversation, floods, or anything that causes ripples or waves in life.

We always learn best through experience and through trial and error, but remember that God can cover us through any and all circumstances. How do I combat the counterattacks? Well, I always *pray and declare* that there will be no transferal of spirits, and that the enemy and his cronies will not harass or torment me, my family, or loved ones in ministry.

COMPASSION AND PASSION

When people are called to the deliverance ministry, they need to have compassion and a passion for those being delivered. Through the years, I've witnessed people who thought they needed to scream at the demon(s) in a person in order for them to hear and for deliverance to come. Honestly, sometimes in deliverances, I do scream. At other times I'm as gentle as the one being delivered. It requires being yielded and sensitive to what the Father is doing in that moment, and how I can best honor the person who is being freed from demonization. I'm to be all things to all people.

Hebrews 2:14 says it all—Jesus came to destroy the devil, and *He did!* From the book of Genesis to Jesus' time on earth to today, this freedom from the enemy has been freely given to us—right here, right now. The enemy may have ten cards up his sleeve, but that's it. He is limited. There are only so many patterns, templates, or tricks that satan can use against us; he just slightly changes them as he reuses them to try and fool us into believing they are something new that you have never dealt with before. I trust in my Jesus, His Word, and the knowledge He has given me through personal experience to defeat the enemy through His resurrection power. We *do* have the keys!

Christian leaders and pastors must know how to counterattack problems in the spirit, yet many leaders are so uneducated in this area. The enemy has worked overtime to convince God's people to refuse to accept deliverance ministry as relevant in our time, and that God is no longer calling the saints to the work of deliverance ministry. The enemy wants us to water down the Word of God until we question other gifts and authority, like, "If deliverance isn't real, maybe speaking in tongues is nothing but manmade sounds?" We know this isn't true; the gift of tongues is real—it's our heavenly language, and not only a gift, but a powerful weapon.

Please understand that I am not advocating every deliverance ministry and methodology. There are many great men and woman doing extraordinary deliverances and great works. But there are also deliverance methods being used that are borderline abusive, that leave people crippled and in worse condition than before the deliverance began. I would liken these methods to a form of domestic violence in the deliverance. Or people are charging money for it. I think of the story in Acts 19:11-15 (NIV):

> *God did extraordinary miracles through Paul, so that even handkerchiefs and aprons that had touched him were taken to the sick, and their illnesses were cured and the evil spirits left them. Some Jews who went around driving out evil spirits tried to invoke the name of the Lord Jesus over those who were demon-possessed. They would say, "In the name of the Jesus whom Paul preaches, I command you to come out." Seven sons of Sceva, a*

Jewish chief priest, were doing this. One day the evil spirit answered them, "Jesus I know, and Paul I know about, but who are you?" Then the man who had the evil spirit jumped on them and overpowered them all. He gave them such a beating that they ran out of the house naked and bleeding.

I have met many people through the years with unbelievable stories of "botched" deliverances at the hands of both ministers and laypersons. Some of these individuals were led to think that they were clinically insane. One woman told me of a pastor who, while conducting deliverance, hit her in the face with his Bible. The force of the impact knocked out three of her teeth. This really frightens me! We wonder why many of God's people are bound, wounded, and confused, suffering from thoughts of insecurity and believing they will never be good enough. They have heard the Word of God and believe it to be true, yet they continue to suffer through major trauma and catastrophe in their lives. Many are crippled and want to give up, but I pray you will join me and we will fight and bring them home.

Leaders must be careful to discern each case individually, for many of God's sheep are scared and alone. They are POWs (prisoners of war), MIA (missing in action), or COWs (casualties of war). Every month I travel to different locations throughout the world, and I see a commonality everywhere I go—people are imprisoned, missing, wounded, fearful, and hopeless. But it doesn't have to be this way! We have been given all authority; and as we partner with Christ to see demonic strongholds released and freedom for the captives, we *will* see greater works performed on earth than even Jesus Himself did, just as He promised we would.

Instead of offering encouragement God's way, many people like to showcase the demons, normally in a public viewing area, you know, at church or a setting with an audience so they can talk to the spirits, etc. As for me, I live by a code taken from the Holy Word: 1) I don't talk out loud to demons and call out their names. I find that to be very dangerous. There are times during prayer when the Lord gives me their names and the strongholds that have them bound; 2) All demons are liars, transformers, and deceivers; 3) I have stayed the course faithfully and helped as many as possible.

Knowing how many have been deceived has birthed a desperate need for the deliverance and healing centers we have established. The extreme cases are being helped, and many are being set free. Of course, this all takes time. We must freely give what He has given to us, giving away to help those who are desperate and in need.

PRAYER

I pray that you will flourish in the Lord! That you will finish strong! Holy Spirit, give us clarity, understanding, and wisdom. May you give this reader the grace needed to accomplish all that is on this person's heart, Lord. Give favor as this friend and strength and good health. I pray that favor will increase in every place this believer walks. Right now, in the name of Jesus, I pray against any demonic interference with "the fruit that remains" (John 15:5). Thank You, Lord!

Chapter 8

POWER OVER SATAN AND DEMONS

In fact, no one can enter a strong man's house without first tying him up. Then he can plunder the strong man's house (Mark 3:27 NIV).

THIS VERSE IS TELLING US THAT YES; WE CAN DEFEAT SATAN BY tying up the forces of darkness, robbing their "house," and setting free those who are enslaved by him. The evil of satan must be driven out. Throughout the New Testament we read of how many suffered from satan's oppression and influence because of the indwelling of evil spirits. Demons are spirit beings that have personalities and are intelligent (Greek: daimonion or evil spirits). Just as God has a spiritual order, so does satan.

*When the unclean spirit is **gone out** of a man, he **walked** through dry places, **seeking** rest, and **found** none. Then he **said, I will** return into my house from whence **I came out**; and **when he is come, he found it** empty, swept, and* *garnished. Then he goes and* **takes** *with himself seven* **other spirits** *more wicked than himself, and they* **enter in and dwell there**: *and the last state of that man is worse than the first. Even so shall it be also unto this wicked generation* (Matthew 12:43-45 KJV).

There are twelve manifestations and or attributes of an unclean spirit that are seen in Matthew 12:43-45. The number 12 signifies government or authority. We see here how the unclean spirit responded to being removed, and the lengths it was willing to go to return.

Demons are the power behind idol gods. Unfortunately, many Christians are deceived by not knowing the true nature of Christ. Demons can and do live in unbelievers. In Mark 5:12, we see that demons have the ability to speak; they channel their voices through their victims: *"So all the devils begged Him, saying, 'Send us to the swine, that we may enter them.'"* We must be very careful what we allow to influence us in areas of media, including television, music, and reading material. Every choice has a consequence. Our souls can be affected by demonic influence, directing our thoughts, emotions, and actions. This is why we must guard our hearts and minds.

Of course, in these last days, evil spirits will be promoting more violence, immorality, greed, and acceptance of occult activity. Even Wicca is recognized as a religion and has IRS status. We will see more evil released on the big screens, television, magazines, and music. We have become so desensitized that we consider there to be no harm in permitting these actions to take place. We forget that we *do* have a voice and need to start crying out just as Mordecai did when a decree was issued to kill all the Jews. This was with a pure fast and mourning, crying out to the Father because they had sinned against the Lord their God.

I believe we are at a time when we need to cry out by fasting and with sackcloth and ashes to proclaim death to *our* needs and wants, and to pick up *His* needs. We are no different in many areas than our ancestors. Yes, we have a great heritage, but the Father is looking for those who will take a stand and not allow the diseased sacrifices to remain on His altar. In Matthew 12:29, Jesus came to earth to bind satan, and set free those enslaved to him, by doing for them what they could not do for themselves. Jesus became the perfect sacrifice. He is the Lamb of God. We have the resurrected power of Jesus to overpower the enemy and destroy the works of darkness. What we do not conquer—face, deal with, process through—will eventually conquer us.

> *But no one can go into a strong man's house and steal his property unless he first overpowers and ties up the strong man, and then he will ransack and rob his house* (Mark 3:27 AMP).

Let us serve notice this day: "*...as for me and my household, we will serve the Lord*" (Joshua 24:15 NIV).

THE CHURCH'S AUTHORITY

We are the church, not the building. That is just a structure. We make up the body of Christ, not doors, windows, or walls. Power and authority have two systems in operation. The first system, power, is *dunamis* as used in Acts 1:8 (AMP):

> *But **you will receive power** and ability when the Holy Spirit comes upon you; and you will be My witnesses [to tell people about Me] both in Jerusalem and in all Judea, and Samaria, and even to the ends of the earth.*

Power is visible.

117

Authority, the second system, is given to us (the *ecclesia*) from Jesus. We have been given *all* authority over the kingdom of darkness. Authority is the power or right to give orders, make decisions, and enforce obedience. In Luke 10:19 (AMP) we read:

> *Listen carefully:* **I have given you authority** *[that you now possess] to tread on serpents and scorpions, and [***the ability to exercise authority****] over all the power of the enemy* (Satan)*; and nothing will [in any way] harm you.*

Authority impacts the darkness; you go from visible to the invisible. You step into a different realm of the spirit.

As you are saved and filled with the Holy Spirit, you have *dunamis* power. You can pray for others and expect to see miracles and healings take place in the natural realm. As you step into the authority given you, you step into the spirit realm. I look at it like a veil that you step through. Power is visible. Authority impacts the darkness from visible to invisible. The Father says throughout His Word that we are to walk in authority. Limitations will come through satan and our carnal nature, but I hear the Father saying right now, "Tell My sons and daughters to take off the limitations! Step over and beyond the limitations you are believing and trust Me and My Word!"

> *In reading this, then, you will be able to understand my insight into the mystery of Christ, which was not made known to people in other generations as it has now been revealed by the Spirit to God's holy apostles and prophets. This mystery is that through the gospel the Gentiles are heirs together with Israel, members together of one body, and sharers together in the promise in Christ Jesus. I became a servant of this gospel by the gift of God's grace given me through the working of his power. Although I am*

less than the least of all the Lord's people, this grace was given me: to preach to the Gentiles the boundless riches of Christ, and to make plain to everyone the administration of this mystery, which for ages past was kept hidden in God, who created all things. **His intent was that now, through the church, the manifold wisdom of God should be made known to the rulers and authorities in the heavenly realms, according to his eternal purpose that he accomplished in Christ Jesus our Lord.** *In him and through faith in him we may approach God with freedom and confidence* (Ephesians 3:4-12 NIV).

See, it is God's will and intent for us, as the church, to combat the ruling powers of darkness in the spiritual realm, proclaiming salvation through spiritual warfare against satan and his cronies. In Daniel 9:2-23, Daniel went into intercession and turned to the Lord God, pleading with Him in prayer and petition, in fasting, and in sackcloth and ashes. *"I set my face toward the Lord God to make request by prayer and supplications, with fasting, sackcloth, and ashes"* (Daniel 9:3).

Unfortunately, many people never get past saying a prayer; they simply don't know how to petition the Lord and hold on until they get their answer: *"The prince of the kingdom of Persia withstood me one and twenty days: but, lo, Michael, one of the chief princes, came to help me; and I remained there with the kings of Persia"* (Daniel 10:13 KJV).

We need to hold on, pray, and wait. I have seen so many defeated brothers and sisters quit and walk away when the pressure is on. Obviously, satan doesn't want you to be victorious. He is always intruding in our Promised Land. When you are at what feels like your weakest point, the enemy will send in his enforcers

119

to attempt to make certain that you do not make it. This is why in ministry many are called, but few are chosen. We must *hold on* until we get our blessings!

> *For this is what the Lord, the God of Israel, says: "The jar of flour will not be used up and the jug of oil will not run dry until the day the Lord sends rain on the land"* (1 Kings 17:14 NIV).

The flour represents the bread of life, which is the Word of God, and the oil is the Holy Spirit, who brings light into the darkness. The Lord will reign on the land, and that is the power of the Holy Spirit in us. As the story goes, Elijah had to stand up against the king and queen, the priests and prophets of that time—and he stood for His God.

Today, God is looking for those who will hear and heed His voice and be obedient, even if it means to separate himself from them and go do something so obscure that it makes no sense. God will take care of you. Are you afraid to go forth into what God has called you to do? Are you standing in a place where He didn't tell you to be? You may be barely holding on, and are only attending church out of habit or obligation. Just know that when your season is over, it's over, and it is alright to pick up and move on. Set us free, Jesus!

Amos 8:11 says, "'The days are coming,' declares the Sovereign Lord, 'when I will send a famine through the land—not a famine of food or a thirst for water, but a famine of hearing the words of the Lord.'" The prophet Amos spoke of a different kind of famine. He called it a famine of not hearing the words of the Lord. We are in a time when Amos's prophecy is coming to pass. We have more revelation and knowledge than any generation, yet people are starving for the intimate knowledge of God. They only know that they are looking for something, not knowing how to access it. God has given us true power through His Word, the authority to multiply, subdue, and take dominion. The true power bubbles up from an intimacy with Him. With His Word we can do all things. We must not take His word for granted. His grace and mercy flows with love and compassion from above.

Knowing who we are and what we are called to do is vital for today's church. Too often men and women of God have become power hungry. It's seen in the media and in their character. Most start out with the right intentions, but, like King Ahab, they end up selling their souls for power, lust, greed. I have seen this throughout the years in my travels.

If as a child we have gone through trauma or been overlooked, we might believe other people's opinions of ourselves instead of God's. I see many times that those behind the pulpits would be better off elsewhere. People who are wounded sometimes seek validation by holding positions of power rather than positions that fit God's destiny for them. This can often cause people to not be in the correct position on the wall or battle line where they belong. We have negated the lesser gifts as nothing, as though they're not important. It is important to remember that *all* the gifts are from the Holy Spirit.

It is also exciting to witness movements where people are choosing to walk in the fullness of the Holy Spirit, both inside and outside of the church walls. There was a time when people did not believe in speaking in tongues and denied knowing that they had a heavenly language. Faith was also treated this way, and I believe a lot of that stemmed from a spirit of haughtiness that entered into many churches and leaders who were operating out of arrogance and control. I really believe that the year 2020 and beyond will release a greater hunger for the truth about spiritual warfare and will pave the way for greater manifestation of His glory released on earth!

LAHORE, PAKISTAN

In March 2017, I was in Lahore, Pakistan. It was my eighth trip there. I appreciate the opportunity to teach and equip the many beautiful people in that nation. Since 2005, AGM (Angela Greenig Ministries) has been establishing churches, Bible colleges, and orphanages there. This trip in particular stands out—as it was one of the most eye-opening experiences I have had in more than thirty-five years of ministry.

The atmosphere was very unusual this weekend of Purim. Saturday morning I went to our media studio with Bishop Yaqub; as we were filming, the electricity went out. So we decided to sit outside for the interview. Halfway through the interview, we heard gunshots all around us. He was nervous for me and I told him, "Son, if you die, I will bring you back from death to life because I can! And if I die, I will bring myself back because I know I can!"

I am here to tell you that you can too! We do not need to fear the enemy, God is in control! One day one of our pastors was on his motorcycle driving to an Afghanistan border to preach. It is so very dangerous there, and on his way he was shot four times in the back. Yet that same day he was back up and running full throttle for the Kingdom of God. He was and is a miracle. The Bible says:

> *For Christ must reign [as King] until He has put all His enemies under His feet. The last enemy to be abolished and put to an end is death* (1 Corinthians 15:25-26 AMP).

> *...The Lord is my fortress, protecting me from danger, so why should I tremble?* (Psalm 27:1 NLT)

Back to the evening in March 2017—the one that changed my outlook on life forever. There was a Muslim woman who gave her whole life to Jesus. Dismissed by her religion, family, and friends, her former life was behind her. Someone presented the gospel of Jesus, and she gave her all to Jesus; she was now a Christian, saved for close to three months. The pressure from family, friends, and the government for her to return to her Muslim roots and renounce Christ was intense. She said, "No, I will not, I cannot. He is the true Son of the Living God." With pressure mounting and the threat of death looming, they gave her one more chance to recant her Christian faith. Her reply was, "I have met Jesus. He is real. I will never renounce Him."

Later during the night of Purim, in the public square a few doors away from my hotel, the woman was hung and she died—an example to others not to leave the Muslim faith. This is what will happen when someone walks away from the culture there in Pakistan. Before landing, a flight attendant announces what will happen if passengers bring or get caught selling drugs, or if you speak against the Koran or Allah. It is simply stated that if anyone does so they will be arrested. And if caught again, within days an arrest will be made—and worse.

After the hanging, I cried as the words from the flight announcement rung in my ears. I couldn't sleep. I was so overwhelmed that I pounded my fist on the floor crying out, "Lord, why? Why!" I understood the sacrifice in part to some extent; but honestly, why did she have to die while I was there? If you know me you would think, *Angela will say something,* but I could not. I hate injustice and know that I have a voice, but in that situation I had no words. After a while a peace came to rest upon me. God gave me clearer understanding that this woman was a prophetic voice to the people, with a bold witness that Jesus *is* the Messiah; the Son of God.

This was proclaimed to her family, friends, and to the leaders and all the people of her nation.

"So shall My word be that goes out from My mouth; it shall not return to Me void, but it shall accomplish what I please [purpose], and it shall prosper in the thing for which I sent it" (Isaiah 55:11). That is what the woman did by taking a stand and believing God at His word. I'm stirred with a fire and a renewed sense of how powerful we as a united voice can be—and continue thinking about her. I will never forget the sacrifice she made for her King, our King! A voice calling out in the wilderness, "Prepare the way of the Lord!"

The following day, after preaching in the churches, I visited a ten-mile long gypsy encampment in the slums. The conditions were unbearable. The lack of sanitation, clean water, and the poverty were gut-wrenching! I have been to many such places, but these precious people and the weight of God's love for them especially touched my heart. That day the Lord spoke to me and asked me if I would be a voice for Him to the people, and to take on this task. My response was, "Yes Lord, I will."

On this trip I was determined to have wells dug in honor of the woman who was hung. That very day, two wells for clean water to drink were in operation, with God's help. The wells were dedicated to the most courageous woman whom I never had the chance to meet. One day I will. Her voice echoes within my very being. I wanted to share this with you for one reason. You too are a force of Holy Spirit fire, and with each step you take, darkness has to bow, BAM, every time! We have access to so much power and authority—yet many don't walk in it because they have not learned to believe in their strength through Christ.

In 2018 I returned to Pakistan by myself because, sadly, many people fear to go to that region of the world. Yet I know the power of God's word as I have seen it in action time and time again. When

I have called for more angels to come, they come. The angelic await our orders as the sons and daughters of God.

This I ask you: If not you, then who? Will you be a voice for Jesus, going into the dark to stand against tyranny, darkness, and the lies of the enemy? I shared this story with you for one reason, to proclaim that you are a force of Holy Spirit fire! With every step you take, darkness will slink and slither away. You have so much power and authority. You got this! Whatever you are doing for God, do with all your heart. God will lead and guide you through whatever the situation may be.

Chapter 9

HIERARCHY OF
DEMONIC STRONGHOLDS

THE FOLLOWING PASSAGE IN EPHESIANS WAS CITED IN CHAPTER 4, but I believe that it is so important that it's repeated here with a different focus.

THE HIERARCHY OF SATAN'S KINGDOM

Ephesians 6:10-20 (NIV) in conjunction with Mark 5:1-3 reveals wisdom keys that unlock truths and also will protect you and your loved ones:

> *Finally, be strong in the Lord and in his mighty power. Put on the full armor of God, so that you can take your stand against the **devil's schemes**. For our struggle is **not against flesh and blood**, but against the rulers, against the authorities, against **the powers of this dark world and against the spiritual forces of evil** in the heavenly realms. Therefore put on the full armor of God, so that*

127

*when the day of evil comes, you may be able to stand your ground, and after you have done everything, to stand. Stand firm then, with the belt of truth buckled around your waist, with the breastplate of righteousness in place, and with your feet fitted with the readiness that comes from the gospel of peace. In addition to all this, take up the shield of faith, with which you can extinguish all the **flaming arrows of the evil one**. Take the helmet of salvation and the sword of the Spirit, which is the word of God. And pray in the Spirit on all occasions with all kinds of prayers and requests. With this in mind, be alert and always keep on praying for all the Lord's people. Pray also for me, that whenever I speak, words may be given me so that I will fearlessly make known the mystery of the gospel, for which I am an ambassador in chains. Pray that I may declare it fearlessly, as I should.*

Let's take a deeper look to understand what and how Ephesians 6 breaks down.

Principalities—Territories ruled by a prince or from which such a title is derived. The position, authority, or jurisdiction of a prince; sovereignty. They rule over nations in a military structure where satan is their master and they are his generals; the four ancient of days. We see how the darkness was sent in to cover regions.

Powers—Specific capacities, faculties, or aptitudes. Strengths or forces exerted or capable of being exerted; might. The abilities or official capacities to exercise control; authority. Forcefulness; effectiveness.

Rulers of Darkness—Monarchs or dictators who rule or govern, exhibiting or stemming from evil characteristics or forces; sinister.

Spirits of Wickedness—Beings inhabiting or embodying a particular place, object, or natural phenomenon with morally objectionable behavior: absent of moral or spiritual values. Wickedness: depravity, plots, sins, inequity and particularly malice. A desire to harm others or to see others suffer; extreme ill will or spite.

Demons—Latin *daemon* evil spirit, divinity, spirit; Greek *daimon*. An evil spirit; a source or agent of evil, harm, distress, or ruin; an attendant power.

I want you to know that throughout the Word of God there are many stories that breakdown how these evil spirits operate, as just mentioned in Ephesians 6:12. I would like you to see the unfolding of how they operated back then in the world, and still today, which we call spiritual mapping.

In Mark 5 there is a blueprint, a spiritual mapping, of what needs to happen when you're going into the gates of your cities to claim God's power and authority. A picture unfolds before you, and you see more clearly what needs to be done, which is part of warfare and deliverance ministries. Remember that you are learning how to identify the strongholds, perhaps in your own life and family for releasing a full-blown outbreak of revival. When we desire change, we fight for it.

Mark 5:1-13 (NIV) says:

> *They went across the lake to the region of the Gerasenes* [principality]. *When Jesus got out of the boat, a man with an impure spirit came from the tombs to meet him. This man lived in the tombs, and no one could bind him anymore, not even with a chain* [rulers of darkness]. *For he had often been chained hand and foot, but he tore the chains apart and broke the irons on his feet. No one was strong enough to subdue him* [power]. *Night and day*

among the tombs and in the hills he would cry out and cut
himself with stones [spirits of wickedness].

When he saw Jesus from a distance, he ran and fell on his
knees in front of him. He shouted at the top of his voice,
"What do you want with me, Jesus, Son of the Most High
God? In God's name don't torture me!" For Jesus had said
to him, "Come out of this man, you impure spirit!"

Then Jesus asked him, "What is your name?"

"My name is Legion," he replied, "for we are many"
[demons]. *And he begged Jesus again and again not to*
send them out of the area.

A large herd of pigs was feeding on the nearby hillside.
The demons begged Jesus, "Send us among the pigs; allow
us to go into them." He gave them permission, and the
impure spirits came out and went into the pigs. The herd,
about two thousand in number, rushed down the steep
bank into the lake and were drowned.

The spirit of wickedness in this Scripture passage has to stay in
a specific area. The pigs went over the hillside into the waters and
drown, but not the demons. Have you ever wondered where the
demons went? The tombs would today be the graveyards.

It says that *"no one could bind him anymore."* Let's break this
story down. The evil was in the man and he dwelt among the dead.
The tombs were like open portals or gateways. Many tried to bind
him, but they could not. I love how people cared enough, with passion, to help him get set free, yet it enabled more demons to enter
into him. Night and day this man cried out, and in his pain he
would cut himself—but when authority steps in, the atmospheres
changes. Everything!

Then the realms shift and suddenly you step through time and space and realize that this is who Christ has called us to be. So much revelation comes through this parable teaching.

Wisdom keys include:

1. Principality

Over the country and location. The Golan Heights is on the east side of the Sea of Galilee and River Jordan. They were Gentile cities. The cultural is predominately Greek and is one of the four principalities in the book of Daniel.

2. Power

Chaos. This power is the author of confusion. In the absence of order, chaos takes precedence. Whenever anyone tried to help this man, a chaotic confusion and fear hit him. Many deliverance ministers and ministries have stopped attempting to help these people all together. Why? Because the countersattacks were brutal, resulting in car accidents, miscarriages, lies that can destroy marriages, families, and entire churches, etc. It causes such damage that many walk away and give up. It is hard work, like anything worthy you may do.

I did not ask for this gift, and at times I say, "Why me? I can't do this. I'm not skilled and smart like others, Lord, they are way more versed." The questions and arguments didn't go far as I knew in my heart that this was the calling He gave me, and I would have to learn, grow, and trust Him to get the job done. But I questioned, what if I mess up, or my family gets attacked? God is a big God, and covers us; we just need to trust that He is who He is. Four years ago I had to do something to multiply and disperse my calling and what I do, so I began releasing strategic deliverance and healing centers. In numerous states and countries, we are able to equip and help people like this man to remove the death clothes and be clothed with a sound mind. That's what Jesus did, and does through us.

3. Rulers of Darkness

The occult dwell in and draw power from the graves. Necromancers and mediums draw their energy from the dark side.

4. Spirits of Wickedness

Spirits that culminate in the region. Somewhere in the chaos and confusion I stopped and asked myself this question, "Lord, what happened to this man before his life ended up in such torment, in a graveyard totally out of his mind? The demons almost destroyed him. Was he cursed by someone? Was a door opened that he shouldn't have stepped through?" Who knows for certain; but one thing is sure, the demons that possessed the man said they did not want to be sent out of the area. Why? They are stronger in their own familiar territory. Authority stepped in. In Luke 10 we read, *"I saw Satan fall..."*, which says it all. That's Kingdom authority, and it trumps demonic activity. The demons obey the elements as the waters, wind, and their master. Even the legions and demons knew that Jesus is the ultimate authority. Demons are not moved by power, they are moved only by authority.

5. Demons

Jesus told Legion (normally 4,000 to 6,000), *"Come out of this man, you impure [evil] spirit!"* Over and over they cried, "Don't send us out of this area." They begged Jesus and said, "Send us among the pigs; allow us to go into them." He did allow them, and they drowned. But the key here is that they needed to stay in their territory. The pigs drowned, but the evil did not.

Satan's hierarchy is incredibly orchestrated. When you go into a city, and God has given you a blueprint of what to do and how to do it, you will have to deal with the hierarchy mentioned in Ephesians 6:12. God will always send an Elijah—a forerunner, a prophet. The prophetic word brings the activation needed to go forward (a for-telling). In deliverance ministry we must be ready. Many times those hurting will jump from ministry to ministry for help, or sometimes to get the answer they want to hear. We must overcome every barrier and roadblock set before us, as leaders, to help and facilitate removing obstacles that have prevented forward movement. Wherever Jesus went, He always stopped for the one.

I see at times believers visually going back and visiting the graveyards of their past, laying flowers at the grave of what used to be, and crying there in mourning for their life, their mistakes, shortcomings, and failures. They visit what once was but bound, and like the man of the tombs they become prisoners of war (POWs).

Prayer

> *I pray, Jesus, to please help me take the time needed for getting built up in your Word, your presence, your power, and authority, so that I may have a clearer understanding of what to do. I can see it, Lord, that I'm helping others be set free, and I thank you right now. I see victory coming up over the horizon. Just as the sun rises every day, so will (whatever you need). Lord, you say, "My Presence will go with you, and I will give you rest" (Exodus 33:14 NIV). You remind me all of the time of how I am your child, favored, loved and given the keys to help others be free. I have no fear, only faith, and I am a fire walking, tongue talking and Holy Spirit filled. In Jesus' name, amen.*

I carry Scripture scrolls, and they go with me everywhere. I just reach in, untie the Word, and read. They are all different, and

I have found them to be a comfort and a lifeline. There are times and places I am called to go that I think, "Oh Lord, I don't want to put you through some foolish test, but really, go there? I will go if you go and lead my steps. Thank you for the Sword, that You will go before me, and your Angels will be there waiting and ready to assist. In your peace and reassurance, I have rest. Amen."

Chapter 10

SIXTEEN DEMONIC STRONGHOLDS

THERE ARE SIXTEEN DEMONIC STRONGHOLDS. THERE ARE ALSO sixteen major and minor prophets in the Old Testament. The following, through extensive research and desperate cries for answers, is what I discovered about each. You must have the presence of the Holy Spirit, His guidance, and God's Holy Word in order to wage spiritual war and emerge victorious. You also need advisors; those who have already faced the giants and can give you intelligence, "intel," to help navigate the situation—so you don't have to reinvent the wheel. I learned how to battle and have great success in expelling demons by realizing that satan always mimics Christ and tries to be a mirror reflection.

Please know that I am like everyone else and my priorities are as they are called to be—God first, then spouse, family, and the ministry. I believe that you will find the answers you are looking for in the next few chapters. I began by becoming familiar with the foundation of these spirits and their fruit. Then, every time I went to take the darkness out, I had the basics and I learned more and more, and little by little my knowledge grew until now when I train and show people of many nations how to pull down and take back what belongs to them.

I want to also point out that the only way I could have gone and done a few of the successful exploits I wrote about was because of years of learning, and making many mistakes. Once I understood, I wanted to help anyone and everyone. Remember, there are many deliverance techniques and ways of doing them. The most important thing I can say to you is to be who you are. As the years have progressed, so have the dos and don'ts. As previously mentioned, one prays this way, another rebukes that way. Sadly, some charge unbearable amounts of money to set people free.

The sixteen demonic spirit strongholds are:

1. Lying Spirit

2. Spirit of Bondage

3. Spirit of Fear

4. Spirit of Heaviness

5. Spirit of Infirmity

6. Spirit of Jealousy

7. Spirit of Haughtiness

8. Spirit of Discord

9. Spirit of Whoredom

10. Seducing Spirit

11. Perverse Spirit

12. Spirit of Divination and Familiar Spirit

13. Antichrist Spirit

14. Unclean Spirit

15. Dumb (mute) and Deaf Spirit

16. Spirit of Lethargy

Let's look at each of these strongholds in detail:

1. LYING SPIRIT

So he said, "I will go out and be a lying spirit in the mouth of all his prophets." And the Lord said, "You shall persuade him and also prevail; go out and do so." Therefore look! The Lord has put a lying spirit in the mouth of these prophets of yours, and the Lord has declared disaster against you (2 Chronicles 18:21-22).

Manifestations:

And for this reason God will send them strong delusion, that they should believe the lie (2 Thessalonians 2:11).

- Lies, strong delusion; statements that deviate from or pervert the truth, to release a false appearance; the spirit "talks too much"

- Suggests; to put (as a thought, plan, or desire) into a person's mind

- Perverts; diverts to a wrong purpose

- Implies; expresses indirectly: hints at

- Assumes; takes as granted or true, though not proved

- Exaggerates; enlarges (as a statement) beyond normal

- Flatters; praises too much or without sincerity

- Curses; prays for harm to come upon someone

- Gossips; habitually reveals personal or sensational facts

- Babbles; talks enthusiastically or excessively

- Mystifies; perplexes the mind of; makes mysterious

- Misleads; leads in a wrong direction or into a mistaken action or belief

- Misrepresents; represents falsely or unfairly

- Deceives; causes to believe an untruth

- Mistakes; makes a wrong judgment of the character or ability of

- Falsifies; alters so as to deceive

- Religious; relating or devoted to an acknowledged ultimate reality or deity

"Therefore thus says the Lord of hosts concerning the prophets: 'Behold, I will feed them with wormwood, and make them drink the water of gall; for from the prophets of Jerusalem profaneness has gone out into all the land.'" *Thus says the Lord of hosts: "Do not listen to the words of the prophets who prophesy to you. They make you worthless; they speak a vision of their own heart, not from the mouth of the Lord. They continually say to those who despise Me, 'The Lord has said, "You shall have peace"'; and to everyone who walks according to the dictates of his own heart, they say, 'No evil shall come upon you'"* (Jeremiah 23:15-17).

The lying spirit is what I refer to as the godfather of the dark underworld. Without the lie, there is nothing. This spirit's job is to steal, kill, and destroy; to annihilate, to kill your calling, and steal your inheritance. One of the tragedies I have seen is that often when new Christians come into the church, they are given strict rules and regulations, causing greater bondage and fear in their lives than before they came to Christ. It isn't because of Christ, because we know His yoke is easy and burden is light. It is more often the religious, lying spirit at work in a church. Too many have sadly watered down the Holy Word, using grace as a crutch. Grace is important, and a gift from God, but so many believers misunderstand what grace truly is.

Whenever I do deliverance, I expect that the lying spirit will always be there trying to stop me. It must be bound and then commanded to shut up. This spirit's true mission is to pervert the truth and will use us to lie, accuse, and blame one another. Often the person needing deliverance will receive mental pictures, seeing things that are not actually there, and hearing what is not actually spoken. Be careful as a deliverance minister. Be aware of your surroundings, your own thoughts and perceptions. Keep in mind what you are there to accomplish—to deliver those out of darkness into the light of Jesus.

We need God's wisdom and understanding as we navigate through these darker times. The enemy's job is to lie, twist, and insinuate in order to remove what the Father has given us. He has given us truth and life, not death and destruction. Without the lie, the enemy has nothing, and that is why it is always important to test every spirit. Unfortunately, there have been numerous marriages, families, ministries, and jobs destroyed by the misunderstandings caused by this spirit.

With every promise that the Father gives us, there will always be opposition to that promise. The calling on many saints' lives have been lost by buying into a lie, just like Adam and Eve in the Garden bought into a lie and lost the promise and God's glory. Once they knew they were naked, it was too late. But that is why Jesus came—to restore us to Himself and the Father. Jesus is our glory, and it is never too late to accept Him as our Lord and Savior.

Perhaps you have gone through a divorce, lost a loved one, or fell away from what you believed. Please know that the calling on your life is yes and amen; it is irrefutable. Remembering your calling and who He created you to be is the ammunition you need to say to the lies, *"No more!"* It is time to remind the enemy of his place, declare the truth out loud, come out of your death clothes, and be whole in Jesus' name!

PRAYER

Pray this prayer with me:

> *Right now, in the name of Jesus, we bind up the lies of the enemy. I curse every word that has had an assignment on it against me with Your truth. You will not take root or cause my name to be destroyed by your lies and deception. Father, I loose faith to arise and scatter the enemy in Jesus' powerful name. Whatever I need this day, I am wearing my belt of truth, as I am armed and dangerous! Father, every time the lies come in and want to mislead me from You, I ask Holy Spirit right now for your help to endure the trial and times until full vindication comes. I refuse to settle for less. I thank You for what You're doing and teaching me. Amen.*

My personal weapon of choice is warring in tongues, using my prayer language. I do pray in English or at times a different language, but I find personally a thrust from the natural to the spiritual realm when I pray in tongues, releasing the angels of heaven to move on my behalf.

2. SPIRIT OF BONDAGE

Bondage is the state of being under the control of another person. People can become imprisoned in every area of their lives; a slave to satan. Every addiction is linked to the spirit of bondage, because they are unable to break free.

> *For you did not receive the spirit of bondage again to fear, but you received the Spirit of adoption by whom we cry out, "Abba, Father"* (Romans 8:15).

> *And that they may come to their senses and escape the snare of the devil, having been taken captive by him to do his will* (2 Timothy 2:26).

Manifestations:

- Causes submission; to commit to the discretion or decision of another or of others

- Forms a yoke; a device that embraces two parts to hold or unite them in position

- Constrains; compel, force, confine

- Enslaves; to make a slave of (also sex slaves, including children)

- Instills dependency; the quality or state of being influenced by or subject to another

- Commands subjection; a person under the authority of another

- Self-doubt; the enemy can plant self-doubt and you begin to second-guess yourself, which is self-sabotaging. *"Such a person is double-minded and unstable in all they do" (James 1:7-8 NIV).*

- Spiritually blind; lacking the fullness of the Holy Spirit. Some denominations believe that speaking in other tongues is of the devil. However, we know this is part of our born-again birthright: *"All of them were filled with the Holy Spirit and began to speak in other tongues as the Spirit enabled them"* (Acts 2:4 NIV).

- Oppressed; burdened psychologically or mentally. *"God anointed Jesus of Nazareth with the Holy Spirit and power, and how he went around doing good and healing all who were under the power of the devil, because God was with him"* (Acts 10:38 NIV). This is our mandate.

- Not saved; in darkness, not yet redeemed. *"For God so loved the world that He gave His only begotten Son, that whoever believes in Him should not perish but have everlasting life. For God did not send His Son into the world to condemn the world, but that the world through Him might be saved. He who believes in Him is not condemned; but he who does not believe is condemned already, because he has not believed in the name of the only begotten Son of God. And this is the condemnation, that the light has come into the world, and men loved darkness rather than light, because their deeds were evil. For everyone practicing evil hates the light and does not come to the light, lest his deeds should be exposed. But he who does the truth comes to the light, that his deeds may be clearly seen, that they have been done in God"* (John 3:16-21).

- *Bitterness;* a feeling of deep and bitter anger and ill will. Bitterness will rob you of your joy and your peace. It leads to either isolation or greater sin. Cain was bitter in his heart toward Abel; being consumed with negativity, he murdered his own brother. *"Another dies in bitterness of soul, never having enjoyed anything good"* (Job 21:25 NIV).

- Compulsive; unable to stop; bound in a sin. *"The evil deeds of the wicked ensnare them; the cords of their sins hold them fast"* (Proverbs 5:22).

- Bound in chains; unable to break free, enslaved addictions. *"For I see that you are full of bitterness and captive to sin"* (Acts 8:23 NIV).

- Human captivity; under the power of another. Sex slaves. *"But I see another law in my members, warring against the law of my mind, and bringing me into captivity to the law of sin which is in my members"* (Romans 7:23). You will see a pattern throughout this book.

A lot of relationships keep victims broken and unable to be free. This is why there is so much domestic violence of battered and abused adults and children. It is everywhere, a plague within our society. I could write volumes on this spirit alone. It is in our churches as well our schools, neighborhoods, and nations. So many come from dysfunctional homes and are like lost children, groping in the dark for their identity, crying out, "Who am I?" They have never really tasted freedom because they have not received the

Spirit of adoption in which they cry out, "Abba Father." I have seen more of God's people whole and healed once they receive revelation of who their heavenly Father is. It is like an umbilical cord in the Spirit that goes from God's heart to theirs.

When you see people struggling with alcohol, drug abuse, or pornography, always remember that it is rooted in spiritual darkness. They are in bondage to this sin. It isn't flesh and blood we fight against; many of these people have opened doors that they do not know how to shut, and they feel powerless. Many keep searching for the answer. If this is you, do not stop—you will find what you need! Continue to walk in love and keep praying for your loved ones because they *will* be set free. Love is powerful and disarms bondages.

> *The Spirit of the Lord is upon Me, because He has anointed Me to preach the gospel to the poor; He has sent Me to heal the brokenhearted, to proclaim liberty to the captives and recovery of sight to the blind, to set at liberty those who are oppressed* (Luke 4:18).

Every shackle and yoke that has been laid on you can be removed. I would remind you first to forgive others and yourself. Many have experienced so much shame. Once you forgive yourself, those chains will fall off and, like Lazarus, you will come forth! No one can disqualify you—except you, yourself.

I keep my heart and attitude in check as much as possible. I have my moments, but I really don't want to be bitter and downright mean. Regrets and guilt are the most powerful weapons the enemy uses to keep us captive to our past. When I get caught in the loop of the past, you know, that rerun that goes over and over in your head, I start decreeing out loud, "No more!" I always come back to the Word; especially I love Deuteronomy 28:6-7 (NIV):

You will be blessed when you come in and blessed when you go out. The Lord will grant that the enemies who rise up against you will be defeated before you. They will come at you from one direction but flee from you in seven.

PRAYER

Father, right now in the name of Jesus Christ, we break free all who have been chained and held in bondage! (Say out loud) Father, I receive the fullness of what the blood of Christ purchased for me at the cross. I refuse to be chained to the past. I refuse to live like this for one more day. I know the enemy wants me defeated, disgusted, and busted, barely getting by, begging for crumbs, because he sees my future. Lord, I am victorious and leading others out of bondage to You. Thank You for leading me to the right people who can help me walk through and get the understanding I need. Thank You, Jesus, I am learning what real love and freedom is. Angels of Heaven, I call forth Heaven's angelic army to annihilate the enemy at every turn. Thank You, Lord, that one day I will help others receive the revelation and the freedom You have given to me. I am a furious force of Your Holy Spirit and I will not be tamed or shut down. In Jesus' name, amen and amen.

3. SPIRIT OF FEAR (ENEMY WITHIN)

The spirit of fear is an emotion experienced in anticipation of some specific pain or danger (fight, flight, freeze, faint). It feeds off of emotions and terrifies the victim. *"For God has not given us the spirit of fear, but of power and of love and of a sound mind* [self-control]" (2 Timothy 1:7).

Manifestations:

- Torment; intense feelings of suffering; acute mental or physical pain. It cripples the mind and body. "There is no fear in love; but perfect love casts out fear, because fear involves torment. But he who fears has not been made perfect in love" (1 John 4:18).

- Fear of death; *"Inasmuch then as the children have partaken of flesh and blood, He Himself likewise shared in the same, that through death He might destroy him who had the power of death, that is, the devil"* (Hebrews 2:14).

- Tension; a state of mental unrest, often with signs of bodily stress

- Stress; a factor that induces bodily or mental tension

- Worry; to feel or express great care or anxiety

- Agitation; to stir up

- Fright; sudden terror; something that is ugly or shocking. *"Fearfulness and trembling have come upon me, and horror has overwhelmed me"* (Psalm 55:5).

- Inferiority complex; feeling of little or less importance, value, or merit. This can hold you from your destiny.

- Horrify; to cause to feel horror; appall, daunt dismay

- Terrify; to fill with terror, frighten, scare, terrorize, startle alarm

- Hysteria; a nervous disorder marked especially by defective emotional control: unmanageable fear or outburst of emotion

- Petrify; to make rigid or inactive (as from fear or awe)

- Bullying or belittle; to make one seem little or less. Not being good enough.

- Fear of people; causes a snare or entrapment. Fear of sharing words in church or things behind the scenes that God has revealed. Fearful of the church's authority so that you shut down or are attacked when you speak. *"Those who flatter their neighbors are spreading nets for their feet"* (Proverbs 29:5 NIV).

- Anxiety; painful uneasiness of mind, usually over an anticipated ill; abnormal apprehension and fear often accompanied by physiological signs (as sweating and increased pulse), by doubt about the nature and reality of the threat itself, and by self-doubt

- Nightmares; a frightening dream; a frightening or horrible experience

- Anorexia nervosa; a serious disorder in eating behavior marked especially by a pathological fear of weight gain leading to faulty eating patterns, malnutrition, and usually excessive weight loss

- Heart attacks; an acute episode of heart disease due to insufficient blood supply to the heart muscle

- Survivors guilt; you made it out but others didn't. Why you? *"People will faint from terror, apprehensive of what is coming on the world, for the heavenly bodies will be shaken"* (Luke 21:26 NIV).

Fear can be very crippling and can manifest itself in many forms in people's lives. Many people are given medicine to help them achieve balance in their brains, sometimes as simple as sleep aids, sometimes heavier. I know many people in my state of Washington who use marijuana for medicinal purposes to ease anxiety and depression since it was legalized in December 2012.

The reason people turn to doctors and medicine is because they feel trapped, like they are stuck in their own minds. Many hospital facilities are designed specifically for bipolar depression and patients suffering with schizophrenia, but in most people's cases this is not necessary. It is estimated that there are around 5.7 million bipolar disorder cases according to the National Institute of Mental Health. They are struggling with debilitating fear—yet God has given us weapons in His Word to help many bound up in chains of fear.

I have never had hands laid on me for any deliverance. Trust me, I had legions. Yet, in my brokenness *I kept crying out to God for help.* In my mind there was such fear! I kept hearing the taunts of my childhood, "You're a waste and no one wants you." Even after I was saved, fear gripped me. At times I would actually have trouble breathing because fear hit my chest so strongly. I would shake and start to get all worked up. I kept thinking about the past.

I believed the lie that I was never going to measure up to anyone's standards—fear of failure and of man—and that I would never be good enough. If I have fear of other people's opinion of me (which most struggl with at some point), the spirit of fear is certain to attempt a "hit and run" on me. It still happens on occasion, but I have learned to be more observant now for these attacks. Fear became like a suffocating blanket. When I began to allow only God to define me, knowing He loved me, it allowed me to keep going. His love is the anecdote. A real love is needed; a Father's love.

I read and studied the Bible daily. After a while, Scripture jumped out at me and I had an "Aha" moment when it all started to make sense. It was a *rhema* word from the living God. That is when the changes began. We have been instructed by the Father to fear no evil, for His rod and staff comfort us (Psalm 23:4). We are also called to fear no one (Matthew 10:26-28). Psalm 34:4 (AMP) is a favorite verse of mine, *"I sought the Lord [on the authority of His word], and He answered me, and delivered me from all my fears."* He will deliver you from *all*—not some—ALL your fears. I know that in my life I still have to combat fear with the sword of faith, as faith is stable, steady, trustworthy, and faithful. I also fight fear with love and the power of God's Word.

Always remember that people are not coming against you, but rather the Jesus *in* you. I love how Isaiah 26:3 in the Amplified Bible reads:

> *You will keep in perfect and constant peace the one whose mind is steadfast [that is, committed and focused on You—in both inclination and character], because he trusts and takes refuge in You [with hope and confident expectation].*

So, it is honestly none of our concern what people may say or think about us. Another part of this fear is rejection. Feeling rejected or left out; unseen and overlooked; not good enough. Many times I've observed in prophetic meetings that people are so desperate for a Word from the Lord that if they don't get one, they open themselves up to demonic spirits who mess with their heads and plant seeds of fear and doubt.

Please understand that it does take time to break from these mindsets. Sometimes we are delivered and set free immediately, with no signs or symptoms remaining. Other times we know that the lies and the demonic oppression and possession are gone, but we need to *continue* walking out of the valley of the shadow of death. In the natural, as you start to climb up and out, as you progress on the mountain, there will be times you will need to stop and rest so that you can allow your breathing to become accustomed to the "altitude." Every person's recovery is different.

If I had allowed some of the words spoken over me by people to cripple and immobilize me, I would have left ministry years ago. Actually, there was a season when I did allow that to happen because my husband and I had not only gone through a separation, but we were divorced for a short time. Talk about crippling fear and rejections! We were inflicted with the fear of others from the horrible things that were spoken to us during and after the divorce. Proverbs 18:21 states that life and death are in the power of the tongue. If our tongue has that much power, it is important that we use it to speak the Word with confidence, in faith, and with love.

The spirit of fear is an oppressor—so we must use our God-given authority and voices to command the enemy to let the oppressed go free. Since my husband and I have a calling by the Father on our lives, we continued to press on and do His will regardless what people thought or said. But it took much watering of God's Word over our hearts and minds to dispel the lies of the enemy. I am happy to say that God brought healing and reconciliation. We are happily married again, to each other!

My words to the Father were, "I've tried to do my share for the Kingdom all these years. Please, Lord, let me just stay home and be a wife and mom." For a time and season God allowed me to stay home, but when the season was over, it was over. I knew that there were multitudes out there waiting for freedom. I've heard it said that more than one hundred people go to hell every second. Every second! I am a soul-winner first and foremost, and I knew at the core of my being that God was not done with me.

When King David went into the battle with Goliath, he had his slingshot, but also his shepherd's rod. Every time it looked as though David would be defeated, he reminded himself of how the Lord gave him victory through previous battles. So when the victory came, David would mark a notch on his staff. In Jude verse 20, the Word decrees that we need to stir up our most holy faith. I praise God that He gave David something as simple as a stone to defeat Goliath.

Although you may feel as if you don't have all that you need where you are right now, like David, God will supply all your needs when you need them. When I started to understand warfare, many years ago, it wasn't poplar, meaning understood or accepted. I had only His Word to get me through, my lifeline to live. The negative remarks and the looks from people were so hard at times to bear, but I had to dwell and soak in His presence to endure. I heard, "In the cave of intimacy, there you will find Me."

I'm a visual person, so I needed something visible to help me through the very rough seasons in my life, both then and still now. So, years ago I got a staff, and at times I had to walk by faith and not by sight. I would look at the notches in my staff and remind myself, "Girl, you got this." I believe David may have done that too. Sometimes when it is you alone, you may need to stir up the fire that burns deep within, and just keep pressing on. My lifeline Scripture is in Jude:

> *Now to Him who is able to keep you from stumbling or falling into sin, and to present you unblemished [blameless and faultless] in the presence of His glory with triumphant joy and unspeakable delight, to the only God our Savior, through Jesus Christ our Lord, be glory, majesty, dominion, and power, before all time and now and forever. Amen* (Jude 24-25 AMP).

Dominion is supreme authority; sovereignty; to put back in order. In Genesis 1:28, God blessed them and said to them, *"Be fruitful and multiply";* increase in number; fill the earth and subdue it. We are called to rule over the earth. To subdue means to bring back under control. That's what deliverance ministry is all about. I hear from God to "Tell them to take their rightful seat of authority. Bring back My Holy Word into subjection." We are called into a higher realm of His supernatural abundance.

Since the first edition of this book was published nearly two decades ago, we have seen thousands of people saved, healed, delivered, and set free. Actually, one of the greatest joys was, and still is, to see so many people picking themselves up, brushing off the debris and death, and pursuing their destinies again. Many times people would say to me, "Angela, if you can go back into ministry, then I know I can." There is always hope, and it's never too late.

Some of the fruit you will see from the spirit of fear include: a person being very critical, judgmental, an overachiever, and suffering with health issues such as chronic pain or a nervous breakdown. This level of vulnerability can make people susceptible to attack by a spirit stronger than the spirit of fear, often the dumb and deaf spirit or infirmity. Responses to fear can lead them into living a dysfunctional lifestyle. I have seen people become so crippled by fear that they retreat and become reclusive, not willing to even leave their homes. The spirit of fear consumes them and they end up in a cave-like existence, not willing to come out. When we start seeing madness set into a person's life, such as schizophrenia or paranoia, we must take authority in Jesus' name and command these spirits to release their grip from that person! I liken it to the second death of a seed. The first "death" was fear, but its roots became deeper until it reproduced itself. This is similar to how a generational curse operates, becoming stronger and stronger.

Is not this the fast that I have chosen: to loose the bonds of wickedness, to undo the heavy burdens, to let the oppressed go free, and that you break every yoke? (Isaiah 58:6)

We are not to fear any evil…

Yea, though I walk through the valley of the shadow of death, I will fear no evil; for you are with me; Your rod and Your staff they comfort me (Psalm 23:4)

…or the reproach of people:

Hear me, you who know what is right, you people who have taken my instruction to heart: Do not fear the reproach of mere mortals or be terrified by their insults (Isaiah 51:7 NIV).

Remember fear as an acronym: FEAR = False Evidence Appearing Real.

PRAYER

Father, right now, in the name of Jesus Christ, I command the spirit of fear to let go. Devil, I walk by faith and not by sight. No matter what my faith is, it will arise, and all of my enemies, You will scatter in Jesus' name. I counter fear with my will and the sword of faith. I know, Lord, that my faith has to have action. Today I take action over the fear that has gripped me. I take the chains that have held me captive, and this day the Lord breaks every one— enabling me to defeat every enemy.

For the word of God is alive and active. Sharper than any double-edged sword, it penetrates even to dividing soul and spirit, joints and marrow; it judges the thoughts and attitudes of the heart (Hebrews 4:12 NIV).

Your sword will cut through all of my fear and insecurities. Thank You, Jesus. Amen!

But now, this is what the Lord says—he who created you, Jacob, he who formed you, Israel: "Do not fear, for I have redeemed you; I have summoned you by name; you are mine. When you pass through the waters, I will be with you; and when you pass through the rivers, they will not sweep over you. When you walk through the fire, you will not be burned; the flames will not set you ablaze. For I am the Lord your God, the Holy One of Israel, your Savior..." (Isaiah 43:1-3 NIV).

4.   SPIRIT OF HEAVINESS

And provide for those who grieve in Zion—to bestow on them a crown of beauty instead of ashes, the oil of joy instead of mourning, and a garment of praise instead of a spirit of despair. They will be called oaks of righteousness, a planting of the Lord for the display of his splendor (Isaiah 61:3 NIV).

Manifestations:

- Depression, the blues; psychological disorder marked especially by sadness, inactivity, difficulty in thinking and concentrating, and feelings of dejection
- Loneliness; the feeling of being without company
- Discouragement; to deprive of courage or confidence

- Hopelessness; not having any desire accompanied by expectation of fulfillment

- Grief; emotional distress caused by or as if by bereavement

- Gluttony; one that eats to excess

- Anorexia; loss of appetite especially when prolonged

- Bulimia; to overeat, then self-induce vomiting

- Obsessive-compulsive; unreasonable fears leading to repetitive behaviors

- Disconnected thoughts; incoherent, unclear

- Lack of a sound mind; inability to think, reason, or understand

- Delusions; deluding or being deluded; a persistent false psychotic belief

- Illusions; mistaken ideas: misconceptions; misleading visual images: hallucinations

- Abandonment; given up on completely: forsaken, deserted

- Rejection; discounted or considered as useless or unsatisfactory

- Suicidal; desire to kill oneself purposely; to commit or attempt suicide

- Low self-esteem; to set a low value on; does not respect, admire, revere

- Melancholia; a mental disorder marked by extreme depression often with delusions, sadness, gloomy

- Dejection; lowness of spirits, downcast

- Pessimism; an inclination to take the least favorable view (as of events) or to expect the worst

- Hypochondria; depression of mind, often centered on imaginary physical ailments

- Brokenhearted; overcome by grief or despair

- Self-tormenting; to cause severe suffering of body or mind

- Voiceless woes; having no voice; not pronounced with voice

All of the manifestations of the spirit of heaviness speak for themselves. Look closely at the definitions, and keep your mind girded with the helmet of salvation, not the thorns of torment. Job 3:26 (NIV) says, *"I have no peace, no quietness; I have no rest, but only turmoil."* In Psalm 69:20 we read, *"Reproach has broken my heart, and I am full of heaviness; I looked for someone to take pity, but there was none; and for comforters, but I found none."*

This teaching is for you if you are going through a season when the spirit of heaviness has been trying to steal all that the Lord has given you. Yes, there are seasons in our lives when we feel lonely. As I write this, I look at the holidays and how many people are so lonely, hurting, and want to die. I know there are many lonely people out there. Please be mindful that everyone experiences times when we grieve or are sad because of the loss of a loved one or a dear friend. When we see someone going through hard times, we must attend to one another more than ever.

My friend lost her husband to cancer a few years ago. She is so strong in the Lord that many people thought she was fine; therefore, not a lot of phone calls or people were checking in with her and her family. People did not realize that she was grieving so deeply inside; she was crying and scared, lost, confused, and angry. I tell you this because there are different processes we have to go through in our lives, and it is okay to grieve and to feel these emotions.

There is another sister in Christ I know who is still in her "death clothes" to this day. It was six or seven years ago when her husband died, but she is still immobilized, crippled, and most days cannot get out of bed. She is frightened and feels alone.

The difference between these two women is not all about faith, but where we are spiritually. It is also about those areas that the Lord has healed, and the areas that He is still working on. Every situation is different; sometimes it takes a year to heal, others may take a lifetime. In the first situation, my friend allowed the Lord to bring healing and restoration to her heart and life in an every-day process. Unfortunately, the second sister, because of being so dependent on her husband for everything, felt like she lost her identity. Since her identity was invested in her husband when he died, she felt like she died along with him.

Many people do not know how to handle depression, turning solely to the medical field or self-medicating, often through destructive means. Some are getting wrapped up in it so tightly that they often need psychiatric help, which can lead to medications. These medications often make people feel worse than they did at the start. *The best medicine is Jesus!* Sure, it's easier said than done, but we have to start somewhere—and there's no better addiction in this world than to be addicted to our heavenly Father. Depression is a brutal, hard habit to break—and yes, it is a habit! Some may not think so, but a habit is something we do daily, even if we do not realize it. It is by far one of the hardest, if not the hardest, habit to break, because we find outlets to medicate depression.

Alcoholics use drinking as a mechanism to cope, and smokers use that to "clear their head." Many use food to ease their depression, which then turns into a form of gluttony. Food can turn a person from mad, sad, or a melancholy state of mind into a euphoric one! How long does it last? Maybe thirty minutes, an hour or two? We eventually fall back into reality and to our vices. Consumption is what many do to battle depression, yet it is so destructive.

The depression that our son went through involved years of medications, being hospitalized for months on end, and this went on for years. It is so scary as a parent. Every place he went for help he was told that his problem was bipolar disorder—which affects about 5.7 million American adults, or about 2.6 percent of the U.S. population 18 and older, according to the National Institute of Mental Health. And this disorder is on the increase. When bipolar was mentioned, we couldn't believe it. After all, he was in a wrestling competition at school and was doing amazingly well. But a door opened and I saw it like Alice in Wonderland—he was in the looking glass and spiraling down the rabbit hole.

As his parents, we were undone. One of the most horrible feelings in the world was to see our son's mental and physical health failing. It took years of unfolding, or peeling that onion, the problem which included several DUI arrests and the consequences of court appearances, jail, and fines. He is doing remarkably well now and taking no medications at all. Does he still have bouts of depression? Yes, but he leans on Jesus and family to get through, and that's where the road to mental health begins. Children as young as 4 and 5 years of age are on medications for related mental and social diseases, when often the cure is just receiving the proper love and attention.

I believe that the Lord has given us doctors and medication to help us. While medication can be the physical partnering with the spiritual, it is important to cooperate with God as He brings healing. In the U.S., treatment with medication for this spirit of heaviness is increasing at an alarming rate. Children as young as 8 or 9 are being prescribed medication for depression, ADHD, bipolar, etc. My personal belief—and I stress this is my own opinion—is that much of this behavior in children is triggered by the growing divorce rate. So many parents have divorced, and the statistics reflect that divorce rates are nearly as high in Christian marriages as non-Christian marriages.

When marriages are on the verge of disaster, parents can become so consumed with their issues that children are often an afterthought. Instead of being present in their children's lives, children are often left to entertain themselves in front of televisions or video games. This can create a sense of emotional abandonment, grief, rejection, and that they do not have a voice. Children then invest themselves into alternate realities through media, which can eventually leave them searching for something real. That's prime territory for the enemy to enter, slowly sowing seeds of deception and attempting to alter the thought patterns and behaviors of children. Once that occurs, everything changes. Children can become unruly or unmanageable. Parents in marital distress may view their children as liabilities rather than assets and heirs.

At times we need to get help from the medical field with the manifestations of this spirit of heaviness; also we should be fasting and in prayer. God, please release Your healing balm, healing the depths of the minds and hearts of Your children—of all ages!

The soul, if not healed, will cause great damage to you and your walk with the Lord. I have asked many people if they are happy in their walk with the Lord. Usually the answers are no. The cycle of a damaged soul will keep you from enjoying true happiness and feeling self-worth! If you are fractured and fragmented by the pains of your past, those wounds can cause a chasm so wide that you will not be able to step over it into your future.

We need to walk in wisdom whenever things become overwhelming so that we do not succumb and allow ourselves to have a breakdown of mind and body. Like Psalm 23 speaks of, it is alright to go through these valleys as long as you *go through* them; do not camp there and make yourself a home. If you feel like you can't press on, reach out for help! Call on God and friends or family when you are going through difficult trials and tribulations. Go to your pastor or someone to whom you can talk. Never be afraid as a Christian to go to a doctor and get help. Remember, we pass *through* the valley of death, and the situations that arise will subside.

For years I have taught about needing "mirror time," which is taking time to look at myself in the mirror, seeing who Christ has made me to be, and embracing it. When the Lord first called me into ministry, He told me to go and bring the lost and hurting to Him. I had only been saved a short time, but He told me to go. I said, "Lord, I can't. I don't speak well, and I'm afraid of rejection and ridicule." I had such a great heaviness on my life during my teen years that I became anorexic and bulimic. I was living in wells of death and despair. The Lord said to me, "Bathroom time, now!" So I went and started talking to myself in the mirror.

As I started to speak aloud what I saw in me, He began to speak over me, "You are an evangelist!" I honestly didn't know what evangelist meant at the time He said it. For the first half hour or so afterward, I laughed and cried, and started speaking aloud the word of God. Out of your heart flows rivers of life, and I was bubbling over! *"Watch over your heart with all diligence, for from it flow the springs of life"* (Proverbs 4:23 (AMP).

The true mission of the spirit of heaviness is to rob you of your blessings and your joy. Why do you think we see so many unhealthy looking people around us, whether overweight or underweight, or just generally looking unwell? It is because there is an imbalance caused by the spirit of heaviness; first it affects the mind of the person, then the body. Isaiah 61:3 declares of the oil of joy and the garments of praise. It is important that our focus is on rejoicing in the Lord, and we must choose life, not death. Find Scriptures that bring life to your situation and meditate on them, and the enemy won't have a foothold to stand on: *"However, do not rejoice that the spirits submit to you, but rejoice that your names are written in heaven"* (Luke 10:20 NIV).

Depression and lethargy go hand in hand, as both are heavy spirits that can lie upon a person for days, weeks, months, and sadly sometimes years. It's easy to get caught up in the routine of either one of these, because it tends to consume us as individuals, which can be a hindrance to those around us. Nobody wakes up saying, "I will be sad and depressed today."

I began looking for solutions to these problems. In my research I discovered that the mind is bombarded 60,000 to 80,000 times a day. Experts estimate there are between 2,100 to 2,500 thoughts that bombard our minds every hour. I was very surprised, but then it hit me—years ago we were not exposed to the constant bombarding of negative images. Twenty years ago, we didn't have access at our fingertips to Internet sites, cell phones, and all of the technology we have today.

No wonder many of our young ones are so bound with feeling the heaviness of not being good enough, thin enough, rich enough, etc. The competition is out of control, and it's not healthy at any age. Many people can't stop looking at their Facebook or Instagram accounts to see how many likes they received. It's become an obsessive behavior. I say no, we must reverse that.

It's like the saying, "You are what you eat," which, for this context, would be the bread of God. You take it in and you feel good, but if you are not hungry for the Lord, you will be starving and using worldly things to keep you fed. You can even reason with yourself as to why, but He does not want us to consume things of the world, for in doing so, we often feel depressed, lonely, and suicidal. Anyone imprisoned by any type of slavery should start singing in the midnight hour: Freedom! Freedom! Freedom!

To grant to those who mourn in Zion the following: To give them a turban instead of dust [on their heads, a sign of mourning], the oil of joy instead of mourning, the garment [expressive] of praise instead of a disheartened spirit. So, they will be called the trees of righteousness [strong and magnificent, distinguished for integrity, justice, and right standing with God], the planting of the Lord, that He may be glorified (Isaiah 61:3 AMP).

PRAYER

Please pray: *Lord Jesus, I repent from any unforgiveness, bitterness, or offense toward (name the people), in the name of Jesus. Lord, I choose to forgive (name the people), and as I forgive, I receive Your forgiveness through faith and by my own confession; I break satan's power and hold against me now! No more. I pray this prayer in the power of the Holy Spirit and in the name of Jesus Christ; I bind the spirit of heaviness from operating in my mind, body, or soul any longer, and by the power in the blood of Jesus, I command it to leave me now.*

I release myself fully and totally from any of its residue that would try to remain or hold me down through demonic manifestations and its demonic fruit of sadness, sorrow, laziness, lack of motivation, procrastination, despondency, or shutting me down spiritually, emotionally, or physically.

I bind the spirit of depression, regression, oppression, and fatigue or exhaustion. I curse the Spirit of heaviness and despair and thoughts of suicide or death. I command you to leave me now, for you have no rule over me any longer in the name of Jesus Christ, never to return again! I declare and decree that I am set free, and whom the Son of Man sets free is free indeed. According to Isaiah 61, I receive in exchange a garment of PRAISE for the former garment of heaviness (which is gone) now in Jesus' name. I am completely free from these demon spirits, and by faith I receive this gift of deliverance in Jesus' name. Amen.

If you are dealing with a child or family member, let the devil know that they will not commit suicide, overdose on drugs, or die. They will not be lazy, unproductive, or feel entitled. Fight back every time and serve notice on the darkness whenever it hits, in the name of Jesus. Give them to Christ, and believe that they will serve Him wholeheartedly all the days of their lives. You can't touch them, devil! Speak boldly as their mother, father, husband, wife, etc. Plead the blood of Jesus for their protection, and speak the Word, anointing their room or home with oil; if possible, play worship music and read scriptures for the situation. By the blood of the Lamb and the words of testimony, decree freedom! Amen.

Let's pray:

In Isaiah 54:17, it is written that no weapon will prosper that is formed against me in the caverns of hell.

Father, we join our faith with the fire of the Holy Spirit to take a stand against the power of darkness. In the name of Jesus, we come boldly against every assignment, with all of Heaven backing us up. We stand boldly against the words, actions, curses, and hexes of every witch, warlock, and even Christian, and every curse that will try to hinder us from the call and walk that You have at work in us. I thank You, God, that I am more than a conqueror through Christ Jesus who lives in me, and that nothing is impossible when I pray to believe, I will receive. I thank You right now, Father, for breaking off every satanic assignment in my life. I thank You that nothing will ever take me because You are the Holy Spirit who lives in me. Praise You, Jesus, for the blood that cancels out darkness! You are the only true and living God. In Your name, Jesus, amen.

5.   SPIRIT OF INFIRMITY

*And behold, there was a woman who had a **spirit of infirmity** eighteen years, and was bent over and could in no way raise herself up* (Luke 13:11).

There are times when circumstances in our lives can cause our bodies to shut down and we become sick, stressed, worried, or fearful. If we do not take care of ourselves by exercising, eating healthfully, and getting proper rest, we become vulnerable. This is a significant fact for everyone, but particularly for those who minister in a healing anointing.

Manifestations:

- Colds; bodily disorders popularly associated with chilling; common cold

- Asthma; an often-allergic disorder marked by difficulty in breathing and a cough

- Virus; any of a large group of submicroscopic infectious agents that have an outside coat of protein around a core of RNA or DNA, that can grow and multiply only in living cells, and that cause important diseases in human beings, lower animals, and plants

- Decrepit; broken down with age

- Sinusitis; inflammation of a sinus of the skull

- Arthritis; inflammation of the joints

- Weakened; to make or become weak; enfeeble, debilitate, undermine, sap, cripple, disable

- Withered; to shrivel from or as if from loss of bodily moisture; to lose or cause to lose vitality, force, or freshness. Your physical and spirit can start to lose that life force.

- Paralysis; loss of function and of feeling or the power of voluntary motion

- Crippled; bound and in great pain, immobilized

- Pneumonia; an inflammatory disease of the lungs

- Leprosy; a chronic bacterial disease marked, if not treated, by slow-growing swellings with deformity and loss of sensation of affected parts

- Invalid; a person in usually chronic ill health, bound, not able to take care of themselves

- Fever; a rise in body temperature above the normal; a disease of which this is a chief symptom. *"So He stood over her and rebuked the fever, and it left her. And immediately she arose and served them"* (Luke 4:39).

- Blood disorder; an abnormal state the blood. *"And it happened that the father of Publius lay sick of a fever and dysentery. Paul went in to him and prayed, and he laid his hands on him and healed him"* (Acts 28:8).

- Hormones and thyroid; body shuts down, causing physical and mental problems

We must walk in great wisdom. I have had a homeless ministry now for many years, and never once have I been sick. I have had others lay their hands next to mine to receive the Master's healing touch, and I have never caught a cold. I have never had any bug infestation or disease from the conditions we encountered, as some others have.

My first few years of ministry were so hard on my physical body that I would lie in bed with a twisted spine—it looked like a snake, and spiritually it was. It was a physical battle to get dressed, cook, clean, and take care of my home and family, let alone go out and preach. We had other ministries, but the homeless were the core and heartbeat. In those days, before we would prepare and serve about 1,200 people or more, the pain would get so bad. I knew this was not God's will for my life—yet there was a constant bombarding.

I knew that Isaiah 53:3-5 (NIV) decrees about Jesus:

> *He was despised and rejected by mankind, a man of suffering, and familiar with pain. Like one from whom people hide their faces he was despised, and we held him in low esteem. Surely he took up our pain and bore our suffering, yet we considered him punished by God, stricken by him, and afflicted. But he was pierced for our transgressions, he was crushed for our iniquities, the punishment that brought us peace was on him, and by his wounds we are healed.*

So, I would look in the mirror and start prophesying this word. I commanded my body to line up with the Word of God. I was looking back at myself. I had to encourage myself saying, "You got

166

this, girl!" During those few years, I usually walked with a cane or crutches. By the time I arrived and prepared to preach, the fire of God would come upon me, and I was able to preach without pain or aid from a cane or crutches. As soon as I stepped out of the van, I would immediately touch the ground with anointing oil. Everyone passing by would look at me, first in my eyes, and then way above my 5-foot, 5-inch stature, and look at Raphael, my angel, then they knew they could trust me.

I established a blood line and drew my sword in the spirit, letting all know, "You do not want to mess or miss. Want some of this?" People would receive salvation, healing, and freedom. After returning home, I would go back to bed in excruciating pain, but no one ever knew. Particularly for the first three years my body, family, and the ministry were affected from spiritual attacks against us. It was very difficult to endure and to continue in what God had called us to do. After sharing this with an old friend, we prayed together for the witches' curses against us to be broken, and they were.

As I am older now, I make certain that I take care of myself with exercise and vitamins and proper nutrition. We must learn to resist the devil, for he *must* flee, and sickness must as well. I have not had the flu for many years; I believe I have found a key to overcoming disease and sickness.

I have seen far too many deaths in people who should still be alive today, who battled with diseases comingled with lies and fear. If you are dealing with sickness and disease, grab other warriors who are on their knees in prayer, who know the Holy Spirit's voice. Lift up your swords and shields, with graffiti Scripture everywhere, and claim healing! Remember, the Lord knows what we are going through. He too went through horrible hurt, pain, and rejection, being innocent of any and all charges brought forth against Him.

First Peter 5:8 says to *"Be sober, be vigilant; because your adversary the devil walks about like a roaring lion, seeking whom he may devour."* To be vigilant means to be watchful. And James 4:7 states, *"Submit to God. Resist the devil and he will flee from you."* To resist means to withstand, or stand firm.

Luke 10:19 is a favorite verse of mine, which speaks of how we have all the power over the enemy, and nothing will hurt us. When I came across this word years ago, it brought so much freedom to me. I needed to learn how to resist instead of giving up. We must be overcomers through the resurrected power of Jesus Christ. His name means yoke-breaking and burden-removing. Whether hereditary conditions, stress, sicknesses, or a shutdown of the body, nothing will ever separate us from the healing Master's touch.

Christ bore thirty-nine lashes upon His back and body. They tortured him with a multitailed whip with spikes on the tips. Every time He was struck, it tore His flesh, and flesh was pulled from His body, not just his back.

> *He was wounded for our transgressions, He was crushed for our wickedness [our sin, our injustice, our wrongdoing]; the punishment [required] for our well-being fell on Him, and by His stripes* (wounds) *we are healed* (Isaiah 53:5 AMP).
>
> *Yet in all these things we are more than conquerors through Him who loved us* (Romans 8:37).

We may quote these Scriptures from memory, but do we truly believe what they say? If not, we should, because we really are healed and conquerors!

PRAYER

Lord Jesus, I repent from any bitterness or offense toward (name the people) in Your name. Lord, I choose to forgive (name the people), and as I forgive, I receive Your forgiveness through faith and by my own confession; I break satan's power and hold against me now in Jesus' name. I pray this prayer in the power of the Holy Spirit, and in the name of Jesus Christ, I bind the spirit of infirmity from operating any longer in my physical body. I cast this spirit out of my body now by the power in the blood of Jesus. I command every demon of sickness, disease, physical pain, as well as emotional pain, scars, and trauma that may have attached to this demon of infirmity to leave me now. I command that every symptom, negative effect, or residue from this demon to be cast out of every area of my body now and never to return, in the name of Jesus. I confess that I am healed and whole. I thank You, Father, for You have given me total victory and authority through Your name to cast out demons. I thank You for the full manifestation of total healing in my spirit, soul, and body, for I know and believe through faith that whom the Son of Man sets free is free indeed. I ask You to fill me now with Your Holy Spirit, and I seal this prayer in the power and by the blood of Jesus Christ. Amen.

He said to them, "Go into all the world and preach the gospel to all creation. Whoever believes and is baptized will be saved, but whoever does not believe will be condemned. And these signs will accompany those who believe: In my name they will drive out demons; they will speak in new tongues; they will pick up snakes with their hands; and when they drink deadly poison, it will not hurt them at all; they will place their hands on sick people, and they will get well" (Mark 16:15-18 NIV).

Father, right now I want to thank You that by Your stripes I am healed. I thank You for healing my mind and body, and that nothing is impossible with You. Thank You, Lord, that when I was discouraged and had no hope, you gave me hope and allowed me to see and believe that my best is in front of me, it's not where I am today or where I've come from. I thank You, Lord, that when I was bound to every demon of addiction, You severed every chain and lock to set me free. It was Your touch that came and severed the chains, and You set me free through the blood. I thank You that when my heart was broken, and I was fractured, You grabbed all the pieces, brought healing and restoration, and You mended me back together to make me stronger than I was before. I thank You, Father, that Your peace, which surpasses all understanding, rests on me today as a mantle of love and grace.

6.   SPIRIT OF JEALOUSY

*If the **spirit of jealousy** comes upon him and he becomes jealous of his wife, who has defiled herself; or if the **spirit of jealousy** comes upon him and he becomes jealous of his wife, although she has not defiled herself* (Numbers 5:14).

Manifestations:

- Jealousy; suspicious of a rival or of one believed to enjoy an advantage; demanding complete devotion

- Coveting; wish, long, or crave for something (especially the property of another person)

- Variance; a difference between conflicting facts or claims or opinions (divides churches and homes)

- Possessive; desires control or occupancy of

- Skepticism; a doubting state of mind; a doctrine that certainty of knowledge cannot be attained; doubt concerning religion

- Vigilant; alertly watchful to avoid danger

- Anger; a strong feeling of displeasure; wrath, ire, rage, fury, indignation. *"But He did not respect Cain and his offering. And Cain was very angry, and his countenance fell. So the Lord said to Cain, 'Why are you angry? And why has your countenance fallen? If you do well, will you not be accepted? And if you do not do well, sin lies at the door. And its desire is for you, but you should rule over it.' Now Cain talked with Abel his brother; and it came to pass, when they were in the field, that Cain rose up against Abel his brother and killed him"* (Genesis 4:5-8).

- Hate; to express or feel extreme enmity; to find distasteful; detest, abhor, abominate, loathe. *"Now Israel loved Joseph more than all his children, because he was the son of his old age. Also he made him a coat of many colors. But when his brothers saw that their father loved him more than all his brothers, they hated him and could not speak peaceably to him"* (Genesis 37:3-4). *"And his brothers said to him, 'Shall you indeed reign over us? Or shall you indeed have dominion over us?' And they*

POWER & AUTHORITY *over* DARKNESS

hated him even more for his dreams and for his words" (Genesis 37:8).

- Murder; the crime of unlawfully killing a person especially with malice aforethought

- Suspicion; the act or an instance of suspecting something wrong without proof; mistrust, uncertainty, doubt, skepticism

- Cruelty; causing pain and suffering to others, people and animals

- Maliciousness; desire to cause injury or distress to another

- Competition; the act of competing; rivalry; contest, match

- Rage; violent and uncontrolled anger; to be furiously angry; to continue out of control

For jealousy is a husband's fury; therefore he will not spare in the day of vengeance (Proverbs 6:34).

The spirit of jealousy seeks to destroy marriages; it provokes to jealously in deceiving a person by insinuating circumstances. It sets the snare with circumstantial evidence. This spirit is a strongman sent from satan. He has great power, with common demons working for him. If we don't see this, we could make a big mistake.

The spirit of jealousy divides friends, families, businesses, and churches. As you see this at work in your life, go to the person who hurt you, or if you have said something about someone without the person knowing you did. Do not allow this spirit to come in and destroy your life. Love is the key; we must walk in love. It's easy to love those who love you, but our true love, Jesus, said we are to love our neighbor as ourselves. You may not always like someone, but you must love the person. The spirit of jealousy must be bound, the fruit cursed, and it must be cast out in the name of Jesus!

Hatred stirs up strife, but love covers all sins (Proverbs 10:12).

Over the years, jealousy has increased—people want what does not belong to them (Genesis 4:5-8), which is coveting. Unfortunately, it is rampant within many churches; the body of Christ is often guilty of breaking the first, second, eighth, ninth, and tenth commandments, which are:

1. You shall have no other gods before Me.

2. You shall not make unto thee any graven image.

8. You shall not steal.

9. You shall not bear false witness against your neighbor.

10. Thou shall not covet your neighbor's house; you shall not covet your neighbor's wife, nor his male servant, nor his female servant, nor his ox, nor his donkey, nor anything that is your neighbor's.

So often our titles or positions become our idols. But when did the mission become the position? Some want to covet their neighbor's anointing and gifts. Sometimes we slander and gossip all in the name of protecting our calling and to be right. We might be tempted to bear false witness against someone because we want what they have, when in retrospect we are insecure and fearful of not being recognized, being left behind or pushed to the side. We think we are not good enough.

I know from being there myself years ago and observing other people, some with celebrity status, and thinking, *Wow, if I were more like them!* But one day I realized that I was grieving the Holy Spirit and holding myself back with envy and low self-esteem. When on life's journey, the road can become what seems like an avalanche of failures and what-ifs—until you step out and over the obstacles. The Father wanted me to use the uncommon gifts and talents that He had given me for prophetic-seer and spiritual warfare. I never felt that I fit in, and then realized one day that I did, just not like everyone else. I had, and have, value—and so do you.

Isaiah 45:1-4 (NIV) tells us:

> *This is what the Lord says to his anointed, to Cyrus, whose right hand I take hold of to subdue nations before him and to strip kings of their armor, to open doors before him so that gates will not be shut: I will go before you and will level the mountains; I will break down gates of bronze and cut through bars of iron. I will give you hidden treasures, riches stored in secret places, so that you may know that I am the Lord, the God of Israel, who summons you by name. For the sake of Jacob my servant, of Israel my chosen, I summon you by name and bestow on you a title of honor, though you do not acknowledge me.*

The lying spirit is the tree; its roots are innertwined, which not only strengthens the tree to withstand the elements, but I look at it like a lay line. They are innerconnected underground, and we don't know how deep or wide it goes. I live in Washington State where there is an abundance of trees. If these demonic spirits are not dealt with, they grow strong within a person before you know it, and the branches are strong. Once the limbs become weighty, they lower to the ground and release seeds, similar to a pine or oak tree. The wind picks up the seed and it takes to flight. The single seed of a lie, after being dormant for a time, may produce jealousy.

Another seed could develop into rage, waiting for something to trigger it. Just like a seed that is planted into the earth in the natural, the ground needs to be watered in order for the seed to grow. Words water seeds, and start to take root. Before long, the next seed is released, and this time it may produce a murderous spirit in the person. Regarding the deliverance and healing centers we have established, we have to stay very intentionally connected with all the changes that are happening in a person's life. When the pressure reaches a boiling point in a person, it can trigger an avalanche of emotions, which can result in germinating murder and mayhem. When lies, deception, and fear are deeply rooted in someone's soul, the person needs deep healing and restoration. Remember that a tiny seed can produce a forest in the right conditions, which is good or bad. Galatians 5:9 says that a little leaven leavens the whole lump.

PRAYER

Father, please help me to see the value You have placed within me. Help me when I see others advance in their roles at the church, jobs, finances, or if their children are good and never in trouble. Lord, help me to appreciate what I have where I am. May I have your eyes, and remember that I celebrate the victories with my family in Christ, and I also hurt when they're having hard times. Thank You, Jesus, for giving me Your heart and Your peace this day. In Jesus' name, amen.

7. SPIRIT OF HAUGHTINESS

Having or showing arrogant superiority to, and disdain of, those one views as unworthy.

*Pride goes before destruction, and a **haughty spirit** before a fall. Better to be of a humble spirit with the lowly, than to divide the spoil with the proud* (Proverbs 16:18-19).

Manifestations:

- Arrogant; having or showing feelings of unwarranted importance out of overbearing pride

- Dictatorial; characteristic of an absolute ruler or absolute rule; having absolute sovereignty

- Controlling; exercise authoritative control or power over

- Overbearing; expecting unquestioning obedience

- Domineering; ruling or exercising power over (somebody) in a cruel and autocratic manner

- Bragging; boastful talk

- Boastful; exhibiting self-importance

- Scornful; expressing extreme contempt; offensive reproach. *"Surely He scorns the scornful, but gives grace to the humble"* (Proverbs 3:34).

- Stiff-necked; haughtily stubborn

- Egotistic; self-righteousness, holier-than-thou, vanity, gossip, exalted feelings

- Snobbish; one who seeks association with persons of higher social position and looks down on those considered inferior

- Lowlife; person of low social status or moral character

- Vain; proud of one's looks or abilities; conceited, narcissistic, vainglorious

- Superior; of greater value or importance

Many times when you are counseling you will find that when people have fear or low self-esteem, they bully people and dictate, or even run others' lives; but in retrospect, they're insecure. They wear a mask to hide behind and have a real struggle for power and to dominate. They don't want to lose it, as they always want to be in control. It has to break somewhere; someone treated them like they treat you.

> *Pride goes before destruction, and a haughty spirit before a fall* (Proverbs 16:18).

This verse says it all. Pride leads ultimately to destruction, and the Lord will not tolerate haughtiness or its fruit. I hate the spirit of haughtiness that many people have picked up and put on; the "holier than thou" attitude. Many people who carry this attribute are so insecure that it's a bullying reaction so no one can really see the hurt and scared person behind the facade. That is not always the case, but it often is.

"*...Your* [God's] *eyes are on the haughty, that You may bring them down*" (2 Samuel 22:28). Haughtiness often leads to slanderous behavior as well. It is unfortunate that people don't realize how often they judge and criticize one another in the name of being right. We must be careful when we allow even a little bit of haughty pride to stir in us. Not all pride is negative, though. For example, if the Lord uses you to bring healing to someone who is blind, you can definitely feel a sense of pride for being able to partner with God in seeing that person healed. Be excited, have joy, and always thank the Lord that He chose to use you, and allowed a medical miracle to come out of you. Amen!

There will be times people will think you're haughty, but sometimes they misunderstand arrogant and haughtiness for confidence that comes though Christ. My husband, Larry, always says about me, "You can't understand Angela. You have to experience her and what she carries, to get it." I like that. I always say I'm not for everyone, but I'm for someone in all my meetings.

PRAYER

I thank You right now, Lord, and I humble myself before You. I ask, according to Your Word in Psalm 139:23-24: "Search me, O God, and know my heart; try me, and know my anxieties; and see if there is any wicked way in me, and lead me in the way everlasting." I will not allow haughtiness, pride, or arrogance to run and ruin my life. I see others that run with it, and sometimes I get caught up in it, but I do not want it, Lord. I only want what You have called and given for me. I thank You right now, Holy Spirit, that You are going to move powerfully, softening my heart so that my eyes will see only You, and I will know the right time and place that You have for me. I will step into my destiny and all will come together. So, I can thank You ahead of time, Lord, for the great things that You have for me, believing that greater things are yet to come this year. In Jesus' name, amen.

8.   SPIRIT OF DISCORD

*A false witness who speaks lies, he that **sows discord** among the brethren* (Proverbs 6:19).

A false witness who pours out lies and a person who stirs up conflict in the community (Proverbs 6:19 NIV).

Manifestations:

- Destructive; causing destruction or much damage

- Hurtful; to feel or cause to feel physical or emotional pain

- Inconsistent; varying; unstable, not steady

- Fickle; marked by erratic changeableness in affections or attachments

- Unstable; lacking stability or fixity or firmness

- Disagreeable; not agreeing with your tastes or expectations

- Unpredictable; impossible to foretell

- Discord; lack of agreement or harmony

- Opposition; action of opposing something with which you disapprove or disagree

- Strife; bitter conflict; heated, often violent

- Clashing; be incompatible; be or come into conflict

- Disharmony; breach between brothers, disrepair

- Division; discord that splits a group. families, churches

- Defamation; to injure or destroy the reputation of by libel or slander; calumniate, denigrate, libel, malign, slander, vilify

- Slander; a false report maliciously uttered and tending to injure the reputation of a person

- Blame; to find fault with; to hold responsible or responsible for; censure, denounce, condemn, criticize

- Censure; the act of blaming or condemning sternly

- Blacklist; a list of persons who are disapproved of and are to be punished or boycotted

- Sarcasm; a cutting or contemptuous remark; ironic criticism or reproach

- Insinuation; to introduce gradually or in a subtle, indirect, or artful way; to imply in a subtle or devious way

- Rebuke; to reprimand sharply, reprove

- Ostracism; to exclude from a group by common consent

When first learning about the spirit of discord, I envisioned it like a clock going back in time so that seeds of division can spread. Every day, as part of my time in prayer, I bind up all lies, the perverse spirit, and the spirit of discord. I bind the lying spirit so that truth will prevail in all situations. The perverse is bound so there will be no twisting of words or actions, or room for offenses to enter in. The binding of the spirit of discord is so that these three spirits are unable to blindside me or my family, friends, or ministry. This spirit never allows lives to continue in peace, but rather seeks to disturb all order and harmony. Its agenda is to break down family relationships and attempts to destroy all things that are good.

In Isaiah 58:12, we are instructed to repair all that has been damaged in relationships: *"Those from among you shall build the old waste places; you shall raise up the foundations of many generations; and you shall be called the Repairer of the Breach, The Restorer of Streets to Dwell In."* Remember, we have been given the gift of reconciliation by the Father to help reconcile people to people, and people to God: *"Now all things are of God, who has reconciled us to Himself through Jesus Christ, and has given us the ministry of reconciliation, that is, that God was in Christ reconciling the world to Himself, not imputing their trespasses to them, and has committed to us the word of reconciliation"* (2 Corinthians 5:18-19).

Remember one thing about this spirit—it loves to twist and pervert the truth. Make sure you are clothed in the armor of God, because an offense opens the door to deception and discord. When we are offended, we must not allow the offense to penetrate us, or we will be deterred from the call that the Lord has ordained for us.

I believe that my personal job, and perhaps for you as well, is to be the plank that leads the captives to walk over to freedom. We are, like the Word says, called to be bridge builders and restore what the enemy has destroyed.

PRAYER

Lord, I see the divisions that are operating here (add in) and I will not allow this spirit any longer to wreak havoc in my (family, life), in Jesus' name. I see the enemy for what it is and is trying to do. I pray that You will destroy this spirit that has been operating against me, and I thank You, Lord, right now, by Your Holy Spirit, that all will be restored that has been destroyed. In Jesus' name, amen.

9. SPIRIT OF WHOREDOM

*My people ask counsel at their stocks, and their staff declareth unto them; for the **spirit of whoredoms** hath caused them to err, and they have gone a whoring from under their God* (Hosea 4:12 KJV).

My people consult a wooden idol, and a diviner's rod speaks to them. A spirit of prostitution leads them astray; they are unfaithful to their God (Hosea 4:12 NIV).

Manifestations:

- Whoredom; consorting with the devil; *"But you trusted in your own beauty, played the harlot because of your fame, and poured out your harlotry on everyone passing by who would have it"* (Ezekiel 16:15).

- Unfaithful; gives love to another

- Backsliding; drop to a lower level, as in one's morals or standards

- Harlotry; offering sexual intercourse for pay; *"You also played the harlot* [whore] *with the Assyrians, because you were insatiable; indeed you played the harlot with them and still were not satisfied"* (Ezekiel 16:28).

- Prostitution; offering sexual intercourse for pay

- Idolatry; the worship of idols; the worship of images that are not God

- Seduce; to persuade to disobedience or disloyalty; to lead astray

- Fornication; consensual sexual intercourse between two persons not married to each other.

- Adulterer/Adulteress; sexual unfaithfulness of a married person (Jezebel, Delilah, Don Juan), divorce

- Homosexual; person practicing homosexuality; having a sexual attraction to those of the same sex

Therefore God also gave them up to uncleanness, in the lusts of their hearts, to dishonor their bodies among themselves, who exchanged the truth of God for the lie, and worshiped and served the creature rather than the Creator, who is blessed forever. Amen. For this reason God gave them up to vile passions. For even their women exchanged the natural use for what is against nature. Likewise also the men, leaving the natural use of the woman, burned in their lust for one another, men with men committing what is shameful, and receiving in themselves the penalty of their error which was due. And even as they did not like to retain God in their knowledge, God gave them over to a debased mind, to do those things which are not fitting; being filled with all unrighteousness, sexual immorality, wickedness, covetousness, maliciousness; full of envy, murder, strife, deceit, evil-mindedness; they are whisperers (Romans 1:24-29).

Sometimes this spirit of whoredom can entrap us in a love of money, the world, food, and even our own bodies. This spirit typically runs together with two or three other spirits: divination and familiar; perverse, and whoredom. If we allow one spirit to stay, like bondage, it will bring in others—it's just a matter of time.

God has given us the ability to identify these spirits by their fruit. James 4:7 says, *"Submit yourself to God, resist the devil, and he will flee."* Again, I'd rather confront the spirit of whoredom with God than to allow it to bring in more problems. Matthew 12:45 reminds us of seven stronger spirits returning to the person, making the person worse. As previously discussed, some spirits also only come out by prayer and fasting. Whenever we learn any new challenge, such as learning to cook or drive a car, we must continually learn and grow, step by step. I feel the same is true when growing in our authority over spirits; we must persevere in the natural realm—prayer and fasting—in order to persevere in the spiritual realm—binding and loosing.

"And I also say to you that you are Peter, and on this rock I will build My church, and the gates of Hades shall not prevail against it. And I will give you the keys of the kingdom of heaven, and whatever you bind on earth will be bound in heaven, and whatever you loose on earth will be loosed in heaven." Then He commanded His disciples that they should tell no one that He was Jesus the Christ (Matthew 16:18-20).

Although the most common definition of a prostitute is someone who exchanges sex for money, a prostitute is also someone who willingly uses his or her talent or abilities in an unworthy way, usually in exchange for something the person desires. If we are not keeping careful watch over our minds and hearts, we can allow our own low self-esteem to drive us to prostitute ourselves. We will find ourselves so desperate for recognition that we are willing to do anything for a position at work, church, or wherever the need is that we desire to have fulfilled.

God's Spirit of Adoption must replace our destructive behavioral patterns. I can attest to this, as I was born illegitimately to my mother, and have seen the fruit of this actively at work in others. The spirit of whoredom is often overlooked, so many brothers and sisters backslide away from God's commandments and statutes. Then they feel they have forfeited their ability to return to God because they don't believe God would receive them back again.

The spirits of lies, whoredom, and bondage need to be bound, and their victims prayed for so the church can see that the lost are found and restored. What is obvious about the spirit of whoredom is that people give themselves over to the things that bind them. For example, look at our marriages: divorce is becoming more and more commonplace. Lies enter and speak into the ear of the married victim to go ahead and flirt with someone at the office, convincing them that it's okay and they aren't hurting anyone. Unfortunately, instead of confronting the areas in our lives that need God's touch the most, we try to fill areas with substitutes. When allowing inordinate affection to grow for a coworker because of a lack of intimacy in the marriage, before long, a full-blown affair develops, which often leads to divorce. Your soul is worth protecting.

PRAYER

Father, I decree Second Peter 1:3: "His divine power has given to us all things that pertain to life and godliness, through the knowledge of Him who called us by glory and virtue." Jesus gave to those who believe the divine exchange: He was rejected we so were accepted; He was wounded and we are healed; He was made poor so we could be made rich, and He died so that we could live. Right now we've released the full blessing. I will not be under the condemnation of the curse that was placed on me or my family, in the name of Jesus. Right now I step up and step into the full blessing that You have called for my life, in the powerful name of Jesus, amen.

My (spouse, child) will come home, in Jesus' name. My children who live in my house will abide by the rules because Jesus rules this house—not lying, perverse spirits. No evil spirits will damage my life or family, rather each will bow to the power of the Holy Spirt and go! Lord, I release and loose healing where there was brokenness and now let restoration begin in my family and me. We will be stronger than ever. Amen!

10. SEDUCING SPIRIT

Now the Spirit expressly says that in the latter times some will depart from the faith, giving heed to seducing spirits and doctrines of demons (1 Timothy 4:1).

The Spirit of God in the Bible clearly says that in the latter times some people will abandon their faith and follow deceiving spirits, things taught by demons. Such teachings come through hypocritical liars, whose consciences have been seared as with a hot iron.

Manifestations:

- Misleads; leads someone in the wrong direction
- Persuades; cause somebody to adopt a certain position, belief, or course of action; twist somebody's arm
- Lures; qualities that attract by seeming to promise some kind of reward
- Entices; provoke someone to do something through promises or persuasion
- Attracts; directed toward itself or oneself
- Seduces; succeed in seducing
- Fascinates; to render motionless, as with a fixed stare or by arousing terror or awe
- Arouses; call forth of emotions, feelings, and responses
- Lustful; driven by lust; preoccupied with or exhibiting lustful desires
- Sears the conscience; scorches

- Tempts; provoke someone to do something through promises or persuasion

- Excites; provoke someone to do something through promises or persuasion

- Interests; power of attracting or holding one's interest because it is unusual or exciting, etc.

- Intrigues; to arouse the interest, desire, or curiosity of

- Defiles; to make filthy, corrupt, to violate the chastity of, to violate the sanctity of, desecrate, dishonor, contaminate, pollute, soil, taint

- Abuse; to put to a wrong use

- Violates; break, disregard; profane, desecrate, take advantage of, interrupt, disturb.

- Commits adultery; sexual unfaithfulness of a married person

- Prostitutes; to offer indiscriminately for sexual activity especially for money

- Homosexuality; someone who practices homosexuality; having a sexual attraction to persons of the same sex

- LGBTQ; lesbian, gay, bisexual, transgender, queer

The seducing spirit and the others mentioned here often seek out people who are the most vulnerable, making for easier access. They are usually teens and young adults involved in the occult or gangs, and are more susceptible; the "weaker link." This spirit's mission is to take captive those whom they seduce and reprogram their minds, seeking to take full control. These spirits are consumed with capturing their victim and never letting go.

I have seen where vulnerable women have been seduced by men who called themselves prophets—but were not—to entice women so they could take advantage of them. By the world's definition, we might call this person a gigolo—a wolf in sheep's clothing. I encountered this very situation in 1997, and was prompted by the Lord to speak truth into a sister-in-Christ's life. Once her eyes were unveiled from the seducing spirit and she could see the truth, they parted ways. For her, the deliverance that set her free was the truth that arrived at the right time.

In this age of technology, the Internet provides such easy access to pornography. Even when people only glimpse, the image is immediately burned into their brains and branded as a permanent imprint. People can easily become ensnared, opening the door to more devious spirits.

As Christians, we must be so careful to protect our families and those we love. This is the same spirit found in Genesis 3:5. The serpent seduced Eve by twisting words to pervert the truth, and pulled Eve in. If you are ministering or counseling people, please be very careful, as this spirit is like a python snake, seeking to swallow you whole. Just like an actual snake, the seducing spirit usually numbs the person from being able to resist the dark forces used by this demon, causing the person to lose the distinction between right and wrong. When you are ministering to a person affected by this spirit, you must take heed and be careful not to fall prey to it as well.

> *Brothers and sisters, if someone is caught in a sin, you who live by the Spirit should restore that person gently. But watch yourselves, or you also may be tempted* (Galatians 6:1 NIV).

The seducing spirit is sent in from satan to perform specific missions, overthrow the victim, and take him or her captive. Of course, once finished, the spirit turns over the victim to many evil spirits; this spirit is considered a forerunner sent to get a person to "bite the fruit" any way possible, just as Eve did. This spirit can seduce someone into having an affair, destroying God's plan for marriages. It can also bring someone into the bondage of drugs, etc. so it can easily sear or burn the conscience. The definition of "sear" is to make callous, withered, hardened.

Pay close attention, notice what fruit is showcasing, and test the spirit to determine if it is of God or not. To test a spirit is to examine the spirit to see if the characteristics of it align with God. If they do not, then it is from the enemy. Don't rush into this! Please take the time to pray, and fast if needed. Almost every time God will show you and give you confirmation. This is what we are to do: bind the strongman, in this case, the seducing spirit, and cast it out in the name of Jesus: *"Or how can one enter a strong man's house and plunder his goods, unless he first binds the strong man? And then he will plunder his house"* (Matthew 12:29).

PRAYER

Father in Heaven, we ask for the families that are not seeing the signs, or do not know how to help their loved ones caught in the lust and perversion of the world, that You bring Your cleanliness and purity to their minds, blot out the images that have seared them, and help them to be clean and pure. In the name of Jesus, we come against the seducing spirit. We pray and bind up all of the influences that have caused them to start, and command them to stop now. This spirit will no longer violate, harass, and draw God's children into the world of seduction. Lord, we ask right now that You will shut the door on everything that would draw them into a spirit full of lust and earthly desires. The blood of Christ now covers every image and heals their minds and hearts. By the name that is above every name, Jesus, we ask, amen.

11. PERVERSE SPIRIT

*The Lord has mingled a **perverse spirit** in her midst; and they have caused Egypt to err in all her work, as a drunken man staggers in his vomit* (Isaiah 19:14).

Manifestations:

- Wounded spirit; causes a breach in one's spirit or heart. Offense opens the door to deception. *"A wholesome tongue is a tree of life, but perverseness in it breaks the spirit"* (Proverbs 15:4).

- Entrapments; take or catch as if in a snare or trap, and twist so that it causes one to hate God. *"He who has a deceitful heart finds no good, and he who has a perverse tongue falls into evil"* (Proverbs 17:20). *"A wicked man accepts a bribe behind the back to pervert the ways of justice"* (Proverbs 17:23).

- Fool; speaks perverse words. *"Better is the poor who walks in his integrity than one who is perverse in his lips, and is a fool"* (Proverbs 19:1). *"The foolishness of a man perverteth his way: and his heart fretteth against the Lord"* (Proverbs 19:3 KJV).

- Despised; to be despised by others. *"He who walks in his uprightness fears the Lord, but he who is perverse in his ways despises Him"* (Proverbs 14:2).

- Lust; to think perverted things about someone. *"Do not lust in your heart after her beauty or let her captivate you with her eyes"* (Proverbs 6:25 NIV).

- Child of the devil; one who perverts the right ways of the Lord. *"You are a child of the devil and an enemy of everything that is right! You are full of all kinds of deceit and trickery. Will you never stop perverting the right ways of the Lord?"* (Acts 13:10 NIV).

- Sexual perversions; homosexuality, prostitution, all sexual deviation. *"Thine eyes shall behold strange women, and thine heart shall utter perverse things"* (Proverbs 23:33 KJV).

- Self-lovers; *"For men shall be lovers of themselves, lovers of money, boasters, proud, blasphemers, disobedient to parents, unthankful, unholy"* (2 Timothy 3:2).

- False teachers; read and reflect on Second Peter 2— pay particular attention to *"But there were also false prophets among the people, even as there will be false teachers among you, who will secretly bring in destructive heresies, even denying the Lord who bought them, and bring on themselves swift destruction"* (2 Peter 2:1). Snake oil peddlers with forked tongues.

- Venomous; extremely poisonous or injurious; producing venom. *"Their wine is the poison of serpents, and the cruel venom of cobras"* (Deuteronomy 32:33).

- Immoral; marked by immorality; deviating from what is considered right or proper or good. *"Anyone who does wrong will be repaid for their wrongs, and there is no favoritism"* (Colossians 3:25 NIV).

- Moody; subject to sharply varying moods. *"My son, fear the Lord and the king; and do not associate with those given to change"* (Proverbs 24:21).

One of the greatest deceptions is a wounded spirit. A manifestation of the perverse spirit is often gaining access in time of trauma. An offense opens the door to deception. Satan's job is to resurrect your past and throw it in your face. Before you know it, you are facing multiple resurrected past offenses. The word spoken from other people, or just enough twisting of this spirit, is all it takes. There is just one bad seed planted, doubt, and then BAM, your soul is wounded and you become distraught, causing the past pain that was gone to rise up again. Once the wounding takes place, it is very easy to become angry, or confusion sets in. Now you are offended, disgusted, and busted. I pray every day against this spirit. Remember, satan wants your mind, will, and your emotions—the entrapment that the enemy has laid out to disqualify all of your healed offenses.

PRAYER

Heavenly Father, right now I speak healing to my wounded soul. I ask that You would reach into my heart and touch the brokenness that lies within. My heart will not let go until You come close and heal my past and current mindset. Forgive me for my harbored unforgiven thoughts as I draw near to You, Lord, right now. Thank You for releasing me and removing every snare and entrapment the enemy has laid out to disqualify me. In Jesus' name, amen.

Romans 1:17-32 says:

For in it the righteousness of God is revealed from faith to faith; as it is written, "The just shall live by faith."

For the wrath of God is revealed from heaven against all ungodliness and unrighteousness of men, who suppress the truth in unrighteousness, because what may be known of God is manifest in them, for God has shown it to them. For since the creation of the world His invisible attributes are clearly seen, being understood by the things that are made, even His eternal power and Godhead, so that they are without excuse, because, although they knew God, they did not glorify Him as God, nor were thankful, but became futile in their thoughts, and their foolish hearts were darkened. Professing to be wise, they became fools, and changed the glory of the incorruptible God into an image made like corruptible man—and birds and four-footed animals and creeping things.

Therefore God also gave them up to uncleanness, in the lusts of their hearts, to dishonor their bodies among themselves, who exchanged the truth of God for the lie, and worshiped and served the creature rather than the Creator, who is blessed forever. Amen.

For this reason God gave them up to vile passions. For even their women exchanged the natural use for what is against nature. Likewise also the men, leaving the natural use of the woman, burned in their lust for one another, men with men committing what is shameful, and receiving in themselves the penalty of their error which was due.

And even as they did not like to retain God in their knowledge, God gave them over to a debased mind, to do those things which are not fitting; being filled with all unrighteousness, sexual immorality, wickedness,

*covetousness, maliciousness; full of envy, murder, strife,
deceit, evil-mindedness; they are whisperers, backbit-
ers, haters of God, violent, proud, boasters, inven-
tors of evil things, disobedient to parents, undiscerning,
untrustworthy, unloving, unforgiving, unmerciful; who,
knowing the righteous judgment of God, that those who
practice such things are deserving of death, not only do the
same but also approve of those who practice them.*

This Scripture in Romans 1 speaks very clearly of the fruits of
a perverse spirit. When you make a true conversion—the decision
to make a total commitment to the Lord—the perverse spirit must
be bound and cast out. In its place the person must be filled with
the Holy Spirit, be submitted to God, and resist evil thoughts every
day. It takes time to realign a lifestyle someone may have lived for a
long time. When we have crossed over, then begins a new life and
walk. A beautiful promise of a lifeline is in Hebrews 13:5 (AMP):

*Let your character [your moral essence, your inner nature]
be free from the love of money [shun greed—be financially ethical], being content with what you have; for He
has said, "I will never [under any circumstances] desert
you [nor give you up nor leave you without support, nor
will I in any degree leave you helpless], nor will I forsake
or let you down or relax My hold on you [assuredly not]!"*

Whatever the situation may be, the answer is to renew the old
thoughts and realign your mind to God's Word. Remember, be
determined to *walk through* the valley of the shadow of death, do
not build, plant, or camp there. It takes time to renew and begin
that walk you have fought for and desired with all your heart, mind,
and soul.

This study of the Bible is key:

Do you not know that the unrighteous will not inherit or have any share in the kingdom of God? Do not be deceived, neither the sexually immoral, nor idolaters, nor adulterers, nor effeminate [by perversion], nor those who participate in homosexuality, nor thieves, nor the greedy, nor drunkards, nor revilers [whose words are used as weapons to abuse, insult, humiliate, intimidate, or slander], nor swindlers will inherit or have any share in the kingdom of God. And such were some of you [before you believed]. But you were washed [by the atoning sacrifice of Christ], you were sanctified [set apart for God, and made holy], you were justified [declared free of guilt] in the name of the Lord Jesus Christ and in the [Holy] Spirit of our God [the source of the believer's new life and changed behavior] (1 Corinthians 6:9-11 AMP).

This list of sins is used by Paul to describe various sinful lifestyles. All such lifestyles are impossible for true believers, who continue to sin but do not live lives of sin.

12. SPIRIT OF DIVINATION AND FAMILIAR SPIRIT

*Then said Saul unto his servants, Seek me a woman that hath a **familiar spirit** that I may go to her, and enquire of her. And his servants said to him, Behold, there is a woman that hath a familiar spirit at Endor* (1 Samuel 28:7 KJV).

Saul then said to his attendants, "Find me a woman who is a medium, so I may go and inquire of her." "There is one in Endor," they said (1 Samuel 28:7 NIV).

Manifestations:

- Diviner; witch or warlock, soothsayer; observer of times, almanac, and horoscopes

- Enchanter; magician, witch, wizard, ones who practice witchcraft and sorcery

- Hypnotist; charmer, medium, consulter with familiar spirits

- Necromancer; one who consults with the dead

- Conjurer; one who commands or summons demons to appear

- Shaman; an animistic, the doctrine that all natural objects and the universe itself have souls, religion of northern Asia having the belief that the mediation between the visible and the spirit worlds are affected by shamans

- Astrologer, stargazer; someone who predicts the future by the positions of the planets and sun and moon. *"You are wearied in the multitude of your counsels; let now the astrologers, the stargazers, and the monthly prognosticators stand up and save you from what shall come upon you"* (Isaiah 47:13).

- Seraphim; images consulted for advice. *"And the angels who did not keep their proper domain, but left their own abode, He has reserved in everlasting chains under darkness for the judgment of the great day"* (Jude 1:6).

- Mutterer; one who communicates with the familiar spirit as if talking to himself, as is often seen in mental institutions. *"And when they say to you, 'Seek those who are mediums and wizards, who whisper and mutter,' should not a people seek their God? Should they seek the dead on behalf of the living?"* (Isaiah 8:19). *"You shall be brought down, you shall speak out of the ground; your speech shall be low, out of the dust; your voice shall be like a medium's, out of the ground; and your speech shall whisper out of the dust"* (Isaiah 29:4).

- Mimicry, pantomiming; a manifestation also of the familiar spirit. *"Those that be near, and those that be far from thee, shall mock thee, which art infamous and much vexed"* (Ezekiel 22:5 KJV).

- Divination; art of obtaining secret knowledge, especially of the future; a pagan counterpart of prophecy. Inspirational divination is by the demon power, whereas genuine prophecy is by the Spirit of God. *"There shall not be found among you anyone who makes his son or his daughter pass through the fire, or one who practices witchcraft, or a soothsayer, or one who interprets omens, or a sorcerer, or one who conjures spells, or a medium, or a spiritist, or one who calls up the dead. For all who do these things are an abomination to the Lord, and because of these abominations the Lord your God drives them out from before you"* (Deuteronomy 18:10-12).

The spirit of divination is hostile. These two spirits are very close to one another and actually help each other. The familiar spirit is known as a personal spirit guide, who is friendly and even on intimate terms with the person it is in contact with—a servant to be summoned at will. It is often passed on in a family, down through generations. Types of props used are: crystal balls, horoscopes, tea leaves, pendulums, Ouija boards, cards, dreams, signs, palm reading, mind reading, and handwriting analysis—anything used to invoke a response or answer.

The spirit of divination also operates through sorcery. Some methods used in sorcery are to recite magic spells, to put someone in a trance, or to place a person under the influence of any evil power supplied by satan, which can inflict demonic soul ties and the violation of an individual, like a raping of the soul.

Those who practice witchcraft and worship satan are in a confederacy with satan, who is the adversary of God and humankind. In Acts 16:16-18, a slave woman had a spirit by which she predicted the future, and worked "miracles" by giving the illusion that she had Paul's anointing. Unfortunately, many of God's children today operate just as this woman did, being tricked by the demonic realm into inviting the spirit of divination into their lives so they can have power, deceiving themselves:

> *Now it happened, as we went to prayer, that a certain slave girl possessed with a spirit of divination met us, who brought her masters much profit by fortune-telling. This girl followed Paul and us, and cried out, saying, "These men are the servants of the Most High God, who proclaim to us the way of salvation." And this she did for many days. But Paul, greatly annoyed, turned and said to the spirit, "I command you in the name of Jesus Christ to come out of her." And he came out that very hour* (Acts 16:16-18).

The familiar spirit is employed by witches, enchanters, warlocks, etc. For example, a witch will use her "familiar," which is a demon who is to obey a witch, often said to assume the form of an animal. These familiars work in the underworld. They are used in a way that many call the "third eye," as they allow the witch or diviner access and insight. They consider these to be spirit guides. As I write this, I grieve in my heart that in the United States of America there are television shows that allow necromancers, those who consult with the dead, to convince countless people week after week into believing that they can speak to the dead. The details they share about the deceased, such as their name, cause of death, etc., are such deception. In America right now there are more than one and a half million witches. That's about the number of Presbyterian Church attendees.

Many television mediums usually look like the kindest and most sincere people, and they only wish to "help people connect" with their deceased loved ones. They are very charismatic and what they are doing is actually channeling the familiar spirit. Many mediums claim to be polytheists, believing they are Christians, and perhaps also Buddhists. They channel the demonic dark powers and demons who are speaking to them, and open themselves to be vessels for the demons to speak through. Let's be clear: God is God and satan is *not*. It is so sad that people seek help from a medium because they are desperate for closure, to know their loved one is safe.

It is very common for people to reach out to psychics, fortune tellers, for direction. Some even perform tarot card readings on television. Again, these people are simply listening to a demon that tells them what to say. Because they read the cards, people swamp 1-900-YOU-LOSE telephone hotlines with calls, spending a fortune to know their fortune; how ironic. People who call psychic hotlines, no matter how innocent their intent may be, open doors to the demonic realm when they call. Even if they are just curious, it is still an opportunity to fall into deception, as the enemy has this gateway so cleverly cloaked. This is why we must heed the words of the Lord and do exactly what He tells us to do—stay away from such sin.

This culture is not at all God's design or intent. If these individuals knew God's culture, they would know Jesus. To know Jesus, they would know peace and hope, because He is both. His love can quiet any problems, any storms in their lives. Unlike the spirit of divination, the prophetic gift helps people realize they are seen and known by the Father. The spirit of divination is a self-serving counterfeit designed as a clever entrapment.

Unfortunately, many of God's children have bought into the lie that it is okay to reach out to mediums and psychics. Desperate people will take desperate measures when they need answers. The Lord told His people in Leviticus 19:31, *"Give no regard to mediums and familiar spirits; do not seek after them, to be defiled by them: I am the Lord your God."* In First Samuel 28:8-16, King Saul goes to a medium desperate to seek direction by bringing back Samuel; but to both their surprise, the Lord allowed Samuel to speak His final judgment to the king:

> *And Saul disguised himself, and put on other raiment, and he went, and two men with him, and they came to the woman by night: and he said, I pray thee, divine unto me by the familiar spirit, and bring me him up, whom I shall name unto thee* (1 Samuel 28:8 KJV).

Remember, we can go directly to the Lord Himself when we need direction!

Breaking Psychic Curses

Every day I bind up the curses spoken over me, my family, and ministries. I will not allow any demonic curse to lay hold of me, in Jesus' name. *It will go! I bind it up!* In the name of Jesus Christ, I break and renounce all curses, spells, and incantations that have been spoken over me, my family, or my ministry. I curse all seeds, spoken words, and command them to dry up and die. I decree and reverse every curse. Every evil altar that has held back my breakthroughs, be dismantled right now, in the name of Jesus. Every demonic power that has cursed my destiny will be destroyed by the power of God's Word and will be null and void.

PRAYER

Make this prayer your own:

> *Father, I decree Second Peter 1:3: "According to His divine power has given unto us all things that pertain to life and godliness through the knowledge of him that caused us to glory and virtue." Jesus gave me the divine exchange: He was rejected we so were accepted; He was wounded and we are healed; He was made poor so we could be made rich, and He died so that we could live. Right now, we've released the full blessing. We will not be under the condemnation of the curse that was placed on me or my family, in the name of Jesus. Right now, we step up and step into the full blessing that You have called for our lives, in the powerful name of Jesus, amen.*

Whenever a person (aka spirit motivating a person) tries to curse me, I pray that their spoken seeds would not even have the ability to fall to the ground and begin to take root. I then release the truth into whatever the situation may be. I pray for the Lord to set them free, so that the person can know Jesus. Most of those in the dark underworld never really get the prayer they need to get set free. We have been privileged to see many come out of the occult and Satanism, and live whole, sound, productive lives.

13.   ANTICHRIST SPIRIT

And every spirit that confesses not that Jesus Christ is come in the flesh is not of God: and this is that spirit of antichrist, whereof ye have heard that it should come; and even now already is it in the world (1 John 4:3 KJV).

Manifestations:

- Rival; one of two or more trying to get what only one can have

- Counter-agent; one who acts in opposition to

- Competitor; one that competes

- Enemy; one that attacks or tries to harm another

- Imposter; attempts to take the place of Jesus: His doctrine, His Deity, and His victory

- Substitutes; other methods of atoning for sin, and for finding acceptance from God

- Claims authority; would bind man to strict man-made laws, no freedom

- Manipulation; attacks and twists what Jesus did for us personally. Attempts to lie about what the blood did for you and me.

- Opposes; the office of a prophet and the priestly office

- Curses; the gifts of God, attributing them to satan

- Suppresses; families, one spouse saved and one not

- Harass and disturbs; times at church; will send in evil intelligent forces to destroy your ministries

- Persecutes; and tries to bring condemnation to man

- Seeks to steal; and take over man's authority in Christ

- Tries to seduce; into error. *"Now the Spirit speaks expressly, that in the latter times some shall depart from the faith, giving heed to seducing spirits, and doctrines of devils"* (1 Timothy 4:1 KJV).

"666" is the mark of the antichrist. Opposition to Christ will come in the form of imposters, seducers, deceivers, and false leaders. Many people believe the spirit of the antichrist is preparing for his soon-coming arrival. The main objective for us as saints is to continue testing the spirits, reviewing the fruit (Galatians 5:22-23), and praying and asking God to reveal His truth to us. Conversely, it is important that we keep an eye out for "wolves in sheep's clothing." Jesus said that many would come in His name, but they won't be. The seducing and antichrist spirit interlink together, which means we must look very closely at the fruit of people. The enemy likes to send in the antichrist spirit to bring confusion and chaos, making it hard to discern if the spirit is from God or satan.

As I travel and preach, I have come across this spirit more often than once. Throughout the years I have been able to disarm the enemy before things got out of hand, because I was able to identify the stronghold, the spirit, and fruit and bind it, and cast it out in Jesus' name. If you see divisions come into the house of God, pay attention to what's going on. I've seen where the knowledge of this spirit can get out of hand, though, where the antichrist spirit is being used as a scapegoat for people's poor decisions, disagreements, or even to promote their personal agendas. As ministers and people of God, we must pray and ask the Lord to reveal who the spirits are, why they have been sent in, what we are to do, and pray for the boldness to do it in right measure. *"Dear friends, do not believe every spirit, but test the spirits to see whether they are from God, because many false prophets have gone out into the world"* (1 John 4:1 NIV).

PRAYER

Father, we need Your help to recognize and discern the antichrist spirit. Father, we thank You for exposure to our own hearts first, and we ask right now for forgiveness for our pettiness. We shall excel in all that You have called and ordained for our lives. The counter-agents here will be just that, a backdraft. Lord, help the people within Your house to discern and expose the agents sent in as sheep but are wolves coming to destroy the church. Arise within each of us, Lord, to become more aware and bolder, to dispel the wicked ones by the power in Jesus' name. Amen.

14. UNCLEAN SPIRIT

Morally or spiritually impure.

When an impure spirit comes out of a person, it goes through arid places seeking rest and does not find it. Then it says, "I will return to the house I left." When it arrives, it finds the house unoccupied, swept clean and put in order. Then it goes and takes with it seven other spirits more wicked than itself, and they go in and live there. And the final condition of that person is worse than the first. That is how it will be with this wicked generation (Matthew 12:43-45 NIV).

Manifestations:

- Dwells in darkness; in the tombs (graveyards) day and night. *"And when He had come out of the boat, immediately there met Him out of the tombs a man with an unclean spirit, who had his dwelling among the tombs; and no one could bind him, not even with chains"* (Mark 5:2-3).

- Insomnia; an inability to sleep; chronic sleeplessness

- Insanity; no sound mind. *"For God has not given us the spirit of fear, but of power and of love and of a sound mind"* (2 Timothy 1:7).

- Cutting; the use of knives, stones, razors, cigarette burns, etc. to inflict pain and mutilation on oneself. *"And always, night and day, he was in the mountains and in the tombs, crying out and cutting himself with stones"* (Mark 5:5).

- Spitting; the act of spitting, forcefully expelling saliva. *"If he who has the discharge spits on him who is clean, then he shall wash his clothes and bathe in water, and be unclean until evening"* (Leviticus 15:8).

- Cancers, tumors; any malignant growth or tumor caused by abnormal and uncontrolled cell division; it may spread to other parts of the body through the lymphatic system or the bloodstream. *"And the priest shall examine the raw flesh and pronounce him to be unclean; for the raw flesh is unclean. It is leprosy"* (Leviticus 13:15).

- Foul smells; of decaying flesh, corpses

- Gangrene; death and decay of tissue caused by loss of blood supply or infection

- Perverted; deprave, debase, debauch, demoralize

- Harmful; physical or mental damage

- Injures; harm, impair, mar, and spoil

- Desecrates; profane

- Defiles; to make filthy; corrupt; to violate the chastity of; to violate the sanctity of

- Pollutes; to make impure

Evil has become so magnified that it is drawing this generation into self-destructive behavior. The unclean spirit is so strong that many people cannot bind it, and no chains can hold it. In some cultures, it is believed that people will even cut or mutilate their bodies to release the evil spirits. In Mark 5:6-9 the spirit told Christ, *"My name is Legion; for we are many."* Jesus said, *"Come out of the man, unclean spirit!"* and they did. I personally believe that every demonic spirit is a liar. I believe that Jesus could ask specific questions, like the spirit's names and numbers because He is God.

I have done numerous deliverances, always being dependent on the Holy Spirit through the word of knowledge. I do not personally feel the need to ask questions of the spirits I'm encountering because I feel God has sent me to help bring deliverance, so I obey Him. I do not need the spirits to answer me.

The more unclean spirits that occupy the body, the worse the state of the victim will be. In November 1993, I prayed for my mother because she had developed a cancerous tumor on her lung. Within three weeks of the first doctor's visit, it had grown from the size of a quarter to the size of a grapefruit. The doctor said that this was medically impossible. One day after church, through prayer, fasting, and mapping out the details—where, how, and why—a friend, my son, and I began to pray over my mother. Within a minute of anointing my mother with oil, she was slain in the Holy Spirit on the floor. As we prayed, a violent prayer language came out of me like never before. My spiritual eyes were able to see the demon of death in her, with its claws in her lung and her throat. Upon commanding it to release her, within a blink of an eye, the most horrible smell came out of her body, like the smell of burnt almonds.

As I looked for the demon that had gripped her, it was gone. The countenance on her face had changed, and we knew the Lord had cast the spirit of death from her. Three weeks later my mother had surgery, the tumor was removed from her right lung and throat, and she fully recovered. The surgery was originally scheduled to only remove the tumor from her lung, as the doctors had not detected there was a tumor in her throat prior to the day of surgery, because no x-rays indicated this. We knew they were to examine her throat as well because God gave me the ability to see where the spirit of death was latched onto her, and that word of knowledge extended her life.

Through this experience, I learned a lot about true warfare, prayer, and fasting, as well as authority in Jesus. I have had the privilege of seeing numerous lives saved and demonic assignments broken, because of the knowledge I've learned and am sharing with you now.

The unclean spirit walks, seeks rest, and finds none. This spirit is not only mobile, but it can see and speak as well. It comes out and will not rest until it returns to its prey—the host person it previously dwelled in. Upon its return, it finds the dwelling has been cleaned up—the soul health of the person is being restored—and the spirit goes out to find seven spirits more wicked than itself to enter the person. Allowing these spirits to return is a free-will choice of the person, the host, but it's likely the person does not realize that the unclean spirit has company with it this time.

It must be understood that this spirit is choosey; it has a direct plan to overthrow, conquer, and win. The unclean spirit and its cohorts are very smart; don't ever underestimate them. Now is the time for God's people to seek the knowledge needed to identify this spirit and help bring freedom to those who are being attacked by it. So many of God's people have perished from a lack of knowledge for so long through fear and ignorance, but it does not have to be this way. We can change today by increasing our knowledge!

I remember the first few times that I read Isaiah 41:10 and how powerful it was, and is: *"Fear not, for I am with you; be not dismayed, for I am your God...."*

> *Ask, and it will be given to you; seek, and you will find; knock, and it will be opened to you. For everyone who asks receives, and he who seeks finds, and to him who knocks it will be opened* (Matthew 7:7-8).

The fear of failure makes a healthy life seem impossible. As you look to your future with uncertainty, your thoughts, your mind, your very being becomes filled with negative possibilities, and then comes those three words, "But what if?" *What if I have cancer? What if I won't be there to see my children graduate or get married? What if I lose my job? What if I'm not good enough? What if...?* Whenever I hear negativity come out of people or from the adversary, many times I keep it to myself—but other times I counter with, "But what if God says this?" "What if it looks bigger than it really is?" "What if it's really not like that?" "What if the devil's just messing with your head to keep you bound with a negative attitude?"

Remember, infirmity and negativity will paralyze and cripple you. Faith, on the other side, always has positive, forward movement to it.

PRAYER

Father, thank You for giving me the authority to destroy the works of the unclean spirit. No longer will it defile me,

my family, or our health! No more will the unclean spirit
poison me, being passed down generations ago. I have
authority in my life over every evil spirit. Jesus, thank
You for the blood that annihilates, makes null and void,
this spirit's power. In Jesus' name, amen!

When I personally pray against this spirit, my weapon is tongues. A violent warfare comes out of me that at times takes people by surprise. I get the job done and to me that's what counts. Many have been healed of cancer and other diseases or problems they're dealing with when I teach on these demonic spirits and how they operate. For many, it's like connecting the dots that forms a picture, brings understanding with clarity, and more importantly, hope and healing.

When God spoke to Abram, He said that he would have descendants. This meant many, many children. Abram still didn't understand, so the angel of the Lord took him outside and said, "Look up, what do you see?" Abram replied, "I see the stars, too many to count." Abram had to see something in the natural, a visual, to believe God's promise. That's the power of His word operating in authority. If you don't know what to do, hang around people who do.

15. DUMB (MUTE) AND DEAF SPIRIT

The dumb (mute) and deaf spirit seizes its victims, taking over their physical bodies, their speech, and their minds. Indications of the presence of these spirits are often made manifest through convulsions and foaming at the mouth, as the spirit is attempting to actually kill its prey. Mark 9:25-26 says:

When Jesus saw that the people came running together,
*He rebuked the unclean spirit, saying to it, "**Deaf and***

dumb spirit, I command you, come out of him and enter him no more!" Then the spirit cried out, convulsed him greatly, and came out of him. And he became as one dead, so that many said, "He is dead."

Manifestations:

- Suicidal tendencies; desire to kill oneself purposely; to commit or attempt suicide, which can feel compelled to drown. *"And often he has thrown him both into the fire and into the water to destroy him. But if you can do anything, have compassion on us, and help us"* (Mark 9:22).

- Mute; unable to speak. In Mark 9:25 (NIV), we see how this one spirit can cause so many different problems. Jesus rebuked the evil spirit as, *"You deaf and mute spirit."* Some other important Scripture references referring to this spirit are: Matthew 12:22-24; Matthew 17:14-18; Luke 11:14-28.

- Seizures; a sudden occurrence (or recurrence) of a disease. *"And wherever it seizes him, it throws him down; he foams at the mouth, gnashes his teeth, and becomes rigid. So I spoke to Your disciples, that they should cast him out, but they could not"* (Mark 9:18).

- Epilepsy; a disorder of the central nervous system characterized by loss of consciousness and convulsions. *"Then they brought him to Him. And when he saw Him, immediately the spirit convulsed him, and he fell on the ground and wallowed, foaming at the mouth"* (Mark 9:20).

- Blindness; lack of sight. *"Then one was brought to Him who was demon-possessed, blind and mute; and He healed him, so that the blind and mute man both spoke and saw"* (Matthew 12:22 NIV).

- Schizophrenia; any of several psychotic disorders characterized by distortions of reality and disturbances of thought and language and withdrawal from social contact

- Madness; disordered in mind; insane; being rash and foolish; furious, enraged

- Convulsions; violent, uncontrollable contractions of muscles

- Eye disease; an abnormal bodily condition that impairs functioning

- Deaf; loss of hearing

- Crying; a fit of weeping

I believe that there is coming a day very soon when believers will walk into mental hospitals and, by the foreshadowing of the Holy Spirit that we possess, many will rise up sound in spirit and mind. We have been given the authority to do this, but it requires continual dependence on God and asking Him to help us overcome our unbelief and be filled with supernatural boldness. I had to ask Jesus to give me faith to do as He did in the Mark 9 example. This is a continual request I make of the Father, as I always want to stay connected in my need for Him. He can help your unbelief, too!

One night on the streets of Seattle, Washington, after feeding roughly 500, a man came up to me without soundness of mind. This man was causing such a disturbance that I asked the Lord what He wanted me to do. He instructed me to bind up the deaf and dumb spirit and command that it let the man go. So I did, and immediately the man fell to the ground, convulsing. My assistant and I began fervently praying over the demonic strongholds attacking him, which I often refer to as "warring." Within what seemed to be a matter of minutes, the man sat up totally whole and had a sound mind. The change in him freaked out many people, especially those who knew him. We gave him coffee, talked with him for a while, led him through the sinner's prayer, and were able to get him into a shelter that night.

This is what I believe the Father really desires us as the church to do—to arise and be vessels through whom He can flow. By being dependent on the Father and willing vessels, we can continue the work that Jesus started, just as He chose to be dependent on the Father in His ministry on earth. Reach for the impossible until it becomes possible.

PRAYER

Lord, thank You right now for giving me the weapons to destroy this spirit assigned to me or my (name them). I know that You are the only answer, as this spirit wants to kill and destroy the blessings You have for me and my family. Together, Lord, You and I will close the gates of our enemies and shut the door where the curse of suicide and fear of death come in. I plead and apply the blood over the doorpost of my mind's eye, in Jesus' name. The death angel will not come to my door. Thank You, Lord, right now for the victory, as I can see over the horizon that it's coming. I will hold on, it's coming. Amen!

16. SPIRIT OF LETHARGY

The Bible speaks of people with this spirit as sluggards. Isaiah 29:10 says, *"For the Lord has poured out on you the spirit of deep sleep, and has closed your eyes, namely, the prophets; and He has covered your heads, namely, the seers."*

Manifestations:

- Laziness, lethargy; disliking activity or exertion; encouraging idleness. *"How long will you slumber, O sluggard? When will you rise from your sleep?"* (Proverbs 6:9). *"Sluggards do not plow in season; so at harvest time they look but find nothing"* (Proverbs 20:4 NIV).

- Unable to read; vision can become blurred

- Closed understanding; fails to understand in part or whole

- Extreme withdrawal, avoiding emotional involvement

- Lacks integrity; won't pay debts; is dishonest

- Begs; solicits for support; asks to obtain free

- Procrastinates; postpones doing what one should be doing. *"Because of laziness the building decays, and through idleness of hands the house leaks"* (Ecclesiastes 10:18).

- Alienates; arouse enmity or indifference in where there had formerly been love, affection, or friendliness

- Destroys communication; seeks to cause a breakdown between people or groups

- Sleeping sickness; lack of energy or strength causing continual desire to sleep instead of engage in daily life

The lethargic spirit wraps up fear in a sweet package, but with nowhere to go. When the spirit is removed, the person will need to be ministered to in love and will need help in acclimating into daily life.

SPIRITS JOIN FORCES

The following are some examples of these sixteen spirits working in combination, running in packs, and the devastation they leave in their wake. Many people feel the effects of seeds that have fallen from these strongholds and have begun to spring forth in their lives. Through the years in many of the churches that I have attended, I have seen major divisions come through several of these strongholds running together in packs.

I have witnessed how the lying spirit partners with the haughty spirit and the spirit of jealousy, specifically targeting church leaders, giving these spirits control in the church. When these three spirits partner together, I believe their cross-pollination creates a second seed that is planted. Once it takes root and blooms, it leaves devastation in its path. Church leaderships are being attacked by this pack of spirits, and it usually begins by placing their titles on display, believing they are the elite and elect and the only individuals who possess the ability to properly run the church. These spirits often target leaders who are vulnerable, specifically leaders who have felt pushed aside or left behind, or that they are not good enough. Watch for these spirits and their seed, as sabotage is its bloom. The by-product is deadly, and will destroy everything in its path, adversely affecting all the hard work you've done for the Kingdom.

The other extreme is when the lying spirit partners with the spirit of fear and spirit of heaviness. When this occurs, the person attacked responds in the opposite manner, believing they have no abilities worthy of a position, and will never be good enough. This often causes bondage to set in. When people believe a lie, it can open the door for them to be fearful of other people and their opinions of them.

After the unexpected and horrific tragedy that occurred in the United States on September 11, 2001, people have heightened fears of the plight of America because they don't know what's coming. We have the sword of the Spirit, the word of God, from the Father above, yet many carry the sword of fear from the father below. We must know who we are in Christ, and the resurrected power that He has given us. When you have the lying spirit working with the spirit of bondage, these two spirits gravitate to the spirit of fear. It is my experience that spirits typically run in packs of three, and are always waiting to "cut one another's throat" to take a higher position or rank in the pack.

You may feel that identifying and removing these strongholds seems overwhelming, but it is not. Remember that this is like learning anything in life—it requires focus and persistence. It takes time to become confident in what you discern, determining a course of action, and following through to completion. It is important that, if you are utilizing these skills on the behalf of others, you *must* be called into a deliverance ministry and have a heart for it. It is not like a formula you follow and then you're done; aftercare is needed, and you will be the nurse who the Lord uses to help walk that person back into wholeness in life.

The key in healing and deliverance ministry is being a servant, a donkey, praying and seeking what the Lord would have you do, then knowing where He wants you to stop. Please note that there have been times when I needed to walk the same person through multiple deliverances in stages. I use the illustration of an onion: sometimes we must peel back a layer at a time, or it can be overwhelming. Ask the Lord, and He will reveal to you if additional deliverance is needed.

Bottom line: the time is getting closer and closer to when we are in a real-life battle. You can't go to the mall, a baseball game, or fly in the air without being concerned that you may be bombed, blown up, or shot at. No more than twenty years ago, it was taboo to even mention the devil in a conversation in churches. Or if a video game seemed even a little dark, parents would say, "It's just a game." Cartoons that included violence would be defended, saying they aren't violent; they're just something to entertain kids. Instead of being tolerant and allowing our children access to these things, we need to be teaching them the power of the Holy Spirit; how to pray, prophesy, and evangelize.

PRAYER

Father, I decree a sound mind. Lethargy, I will not be running around, tired, disconnected, lazy, and thinking, Oh well, I will put it off till tomorrow. I serve you notice today and every day that I will get stronger, clearer, more energetic, and I won't put off today anymore. It starts now. Thank You, Jesus. Holy Spirit, take full access every second of this day, if need be, and tonight when I go to bed, and I will see improvement in my positive attitude. Thank You, Jesus. Amen! I will fulfill the day's agenda according to Your will.

Now that we've identified the sixteen strongholds, their fruits, and how they operate, what are you going to do with the knowledge and Scripture revelation you've received? What do you see or discern in yourself and your life? Are there areas that you feel the enemy is targeting in attempts to rob you of your destiny? If so, now is the time to partner with other prayer warriors and ask the Lord to remove the seeds and roots of every stronghold, declaring freedom and healing into those areas of your life! Focus on your potential not your limitations.

Chapter 11

DISCERNMENT AND PRAYERS

DISCERNING OF SPIRITS

Every believer must have this gift, which is to distinguish between spirits.

> *To another the working of miracles, to another prophecy, to another **discerning of spirits**, to other different kinds of tongues, to another the interpretation of tongues* (1 Corinthians 12:10).

This gift is special because it provides us with the ability to judge and discern properly, and ask ourselves the question, "Is it angelic or demonic?" When it comes to people's lives, it is important not to jump and make an assumption about what is affecting them because of what we can see. Although I have been in deliverance ministry for many years, I must still remember that it's not flesh and blood with which I'm dealing.

We are dealing with different spirits attempting, and at times succeeding, to rule over us and operate in areas of our lives.

Regardless of the stronghold or spirit you are trying to identify, first and foremost you must be led by God's Spirit. This means your belief system must align with God's Word. Genesis 1 tells us that God created us in His image. Being made in His image helps us to better understand our own identity, as our characteristics and actions should resemble God's.

To be in an identity crisis means that people are in a state of confusion about who they are. God did not intend for us to become by-products of where we came from. With the help of the Lord and support of family, I was able to break off the yoke of sin, transgression, and iniquity of my life. And not just my life, but for the sake of our children as well. I refused to allow any strongholds to continue afflicting me or transfer to my children or the generations to come; only blessings. This is why we need to help set others free. We are made in God's likeness, but we are transformed through knowing Him intimately. Seeking His face and His righteousness determines our destiny and our breakthroughs.

THE SAME BUT DIFFERENT

Just as no two people are identical, no two deliverances are ever the same, but do know that there can be similarities. Let me explain. When I work with people who have been molested or raped as children, they often show fruit of being overachievers, very controlling, and are usually very well-educated. They do whatever is needed to fill the void the violation left behind, making sure it doesn't happen again. On the inside, these individuals are dying and have a fear of showing what is inside. Shame and control go hand in hand. When a violation of the body like this occurs, sometimes one's natural body can shut down, causing many mental as well as physical illnesses to appear. When this happens, typically the spirits at work are: lying spirit, and spirits of fear, bondage, heaviness, and lethargy.

The lie comes to twist and manipulate, causing fear of any human touch, including those of physical affection. Many marriages are in trouble because this spirit has not yet been removed. It causes friction, which often eventually leads to separation, for the mate feels rejected due to the victim being unable to have a physical relationship. I know this from personal experience, because I was in this position years ago, until the Lord set me free. At this point, not only does the victim remain in bondage, bound and unable to break free, but the spouse becomes a victim as well. Before you know it, there is a web of deceit and destruction all around. That's where I was years ago—you, too, can be free.

You now have the keys of truth, and what you do with them will echo in eternity. Many lives can be set free just by knowing which spirit is affecting you or someone else. Your mind is your greatest investment. So what are you going to put into it? Before my husband gave his life to Christ, for years I used to say, "I'm sleeping with the enemy." But I was rebuked and corrected, and through the Word, I started learning how to pray effectively for him. I did not give up until he met the Lord. The battle really began after he received Christ as his personal Savior, because we found ourselves in a spiritual battle of who was in charge of our household.

> *In the same way the Spirit [comes to us and] helps us in our weakness. We do not know what prayer to offer or how to offer it as we should, but the Spirit Himself [knows our need and at the right time] intercedes on our behalf with sighs and groanings too deep for words. And He who searches the hearts knows what the mind of the Spirit is, because the Spirit intercedes [before God] on*

behalf of God's people in accordance with God's will. And we know [with great confidence] that God [who is deeply concerned about us] causes all things to work together [as a plan] for good for those who love God, to those who are called according to His plan and purpose. For those whom He foreknew [and loved and chose beforehand], He also predestined to be conformed to the image of His Son [and ultimately share in His complete sanctification], so that He would be the firstborn [the most beloved and honored] among many believers (Romans 8:26-29 AMP).

Prayers and How To

There are several important steps to take when we are walking someone out of darkness into light, and I'd like to touch upon those now. Whenever someone is coming for deliverance through our ministry, or is struggling with any level of attack by the enemy, I always follow the following steps:

Gather information.

We sit with the person to get to know him or her personally and briefly gather details about the situation. If underage, I insist we are provided a release form signed by the parents, and I prefer having the parents close by, but not too close. Many people are victims of their own circumstances, but some matters are very delicate and should be treated as such. Therefore, I treat each person with the same respect and confidentiality, regardless of the cause of the affliction the person is struggling with. Remember, the devil plays dirty.

Prepare.

I always come prepared. It is my job to pray, fast, and ask the Lord what is needed. He reveals to me what spirits are to be dealt with and what tools or weapons will be needed. As I begin to pray beforehand, I anoint myself and the room we will be meeting in, asking the Lord to release warrior angels, archangels, to come guard and protect all of us. I then begin to praise, thanking Jesus for granting us His power and authority that we work in. I pray against any counterattacks or transferal of spirits, in the name of Jesus. I declare this protection over my family and those who are with me, that there will be no reclaiming of God's property. *"No weapon formed against you shall prosper, and every tongue which rises against you in judgment You shall condemn. This is the heritage of the servants of the Lord, and their righteousness is from Me,' says the Lord"* (Isaiah 54:17).

Choose a location.

We schedule a time and a place to meet. I always prefer doing the deliverance on holy ground, as in a church, unless it is for deliverance of a house—"house cleaning" when spirits need to be removed from a person's home. Often neutral ground is not wise, so as not to allow transferal of spirits or interference from surrounding spirits. The person facilitating needs to make sure that everything lines up as much as possible with this. Do not allow anyone to manipulate the location, time, etc.

Dig deeper to reveal truth.

When it is time to gather more in-depth details, remind those you are helping to not be afraid or ashamed of what they have gone through. It's vital for them to expose the lies, no matter what they are. Remind them that you are there to help, not condemn them.

One thing that is so awesome about the Lord is that many times even when people don't disclose all the necessary details, due to fear or shame, the Lord will give insight to the hidden things, because His desire is for them to walk in fullness of freedom.

As a pastor in deliverance ministry, often deliverances are not a scheduled occurrence for me. They are typically spontaneous, especially during a time of altar ministry. When that happens, I trust the voice of the Holy Spirit to give me not only the ability to discern spirits, but also a word of knowledge. There have been times when I have scared people with the deep insight the Father chose to reveal to me during these moments. I believe this is so I can pray effectively to see them set free.

Again, in a deliverance setting, I don't ask the spirits their names, how they are doing, or where they come from, although I know some ministers do. I'm not saying whether those ministers are right or wrong, I'm just stating that I never have personally done so. When you are in a deliverance situation, there are times when demons will speak. When this occurs, I command them to shut up. If the person starts levitating, or things start to move around within a room, I command them to put down the object or to stop throwing things around the room. You get the point. We are a command-do unit. We command and they need to do.

Bind and loose the demonic, and infill with Holy Spirit.

Pray and bind up the spirits—lies, perversion, bondage, etc.—in Jesus' name. Curse all fruit and manifestations. For example, someone bound to pornography who feels there is no way out. Then you cast it out by the power of Jesus' name. Remind the spirits that they have no more authority over this person. Whenever someone has gone through deliverance, they need to have the fruit of the Holy Spirit, so pray and anoint them, releasing His love and truth over them. Every time you deal with a spirit, you want to ask the Lord to fill the person with the opposite spirit. For example, if you bind the spirit of bondage, you then need to proclaim the Spirit of Adoption over them, in which they cry out, "Abba, Father!" Also, pray a healing balm over their eyes, minds, and thoughts to protect them, sealing in the work the Lord has done in them. Have the person pray aloud and thank the Lord of Lords, then ask the Lord to shut all doors, covering them with Jesus' blood.

Help each person with maintenance.

Regardless of what the victims have been delivered from, they need to hold fast to what they have received with a proper mindset. Depending on what spirit(s) they were set free from, they may need to be educated about some practical steps to maintain their freedom; for example, they can no longer expose themselves to pornography and drug paraphernalia needs to be removed from the house. If the deliverance was severe, they need aftercare. There are times when people are exhausted for days. At other times, the person may experience headaches or nausea. Personally, either I or a staff member checks in with the person, typically for a few weeks after the deliverance, so we can help disciple them through prayer and the Word. It brings a peace for most, because they know the Lord has sent us to be His hands and bring His love to them.

To get you started, I have included a few short prayers that I use in my own life, which I have found very effective. As the Lord continues to train you, I am confident He will expand your vocabulary and use you as a powerful mouthpiece of authority to break strongholds!

BREAKING PSYCHIC CURSES

In the name of Jesus Christ, I break and renounce all curses, spells, and incantations that have been spoken over me, my family, or my ministry. I curse all seeds (words that have been spoken) and command them to dry up and die. I decree and reverse every curse. Amen.

His divine power has given to us all things that pertain to life and godliness, through the knowledge of Him who called us by glory and virtue (2 Peter 1:3).

Jesus gave us the divine exchange: He was rejected and we were accepted; He was wounded and we are healed. He was made poor so we could be made rich, and He died so we could live. Right now, we've released the full blessing. We will not be under the condemnation, never again under the curse that was placed on us or on our families, in the name of Jesus. Right now, we step up and step into the full blessing that God called for our lives in the powerful name of Jesus.

Whenever a person—the spirit motivating a person—tries to curse us, I pray that their spoken seeds would not even have the ability to fall to the ground and begin to take root. I then release the truth into whatever the situation may be. I pray for the Lord to set them free, so people know Jesus; most of those in the dark underworld never really get the prayer they need to get set free.

We have been privileged to see many come out of the occult and satanism, and live whole, sound, productive lives.

BLOODLINE GENERATIONAL CURSES

Lord Jesus, I lay my life before You. You are my Lord and Savior, and I only want to serve You. I now sever the bind and loose myself (or person you are working with) from all generational curses; from my mother and father's bloodline, wherever the curses entered our family. I release and forgive all those who have done this to my family. I release the blessings of forgiveness and restoration of mind, soul, and body. I thank You that You bring healing and restoration to my whole family.

What is generational? This is hereditary, passed down through family lineage. Ask the Lord to show you when this spirit attached itself to the family, and in what manner. Was it through curses, or an action done? Either way, it will produce evil if not dealt with. I always plead the blood of Jesus around those who are not healed in the family, and continue to praise Him for His faithfulness.

DELIVERANCE QUESTIONS AND HOW TO BE EFFECTIVE

If you were standing right in front of me, I would shake your hand and say, "Welcome to deliverance ministry. You will never be the same again!"

As one called to this ministry, I've learned wisdom keys that unlock the gates of bondage. First of all, the enemy will always go after the weakest link in your family. If you're having trouble with your children, things may seem to get more intense because the enemy wants to keep them bound to himself. But you also can become bound in your thoughts, thinking the situation will never change. Remember, *"For as he thinks in his heart, so is he"* (Proverbs 23:7).

I still remind myself always: *"Death and life are in the power of the tongue, and those who love it and indulge it will eat its fruit and bear the consequences of their words"* (Proverbs 18:21 AMP).

SOUL TIES

Your soul is your mind, will, and emotions. To tie is to bind or knot together. You can have soul ties with people; you can have a soul tie with demons. When you're bound to someone else or thing, you can't get loose or break free. Remember, angels can appear to come as light sent from Heaven, when in reality they are actually demons. Many people who have come out of the occult have told me story after story of the angels that guided them along with their spirit guides. One story still stands out.

A lady I helped, a wiccan, had clout, she was high up in rank and had the power and respect from others. There must have been people praying for her salvation because there came that oh-my-gosh moment when she started to get fearful of the spirit. The Lord intervened and sent a Christian who told her about Jesus and His love for her. The lady wasn't in deliverance, so they called me. All I can say is, when the spirit exposed itself, it was like a hurricane in the room. Grown men were afraid as a poltergeist was evident. Four men tried to hold her down, but they could not. As I approached her, I was kicked so hard that I flew back a few feet. The battle was on!

When I stood up, I told them to let her go. All the men backed up. I called on Bubba and Frank, my angels. Now she was on the floor unable to move. Within minutes I was holding her in my arms as she cried. All I can tell you is that with every deliverance, if you asked me, "Angela, were you afraid?" or "How did everything you say happen?" my response is, "Trust and believe in God's Word. When you decree a thing, it is established. If you don't believe in yourself, who will?"

If you have an unhealthy relationship, the majority of the time you have an unlawful soul tie. Of course, that means your mind, your will, and your emotions are not aligned with God's will. Soul ties are very unhealthy and destructive. Two people with similar interests become attracted to one another, but if that attraction is based on deception and lies, relationships and marriages fall apart and divorce happens. I have seen it over and over again. People think that the grass is greener on the other side but it's a delusion; a smoke screen before your eyes. It's a lie that the enemy feeds you.

When you're dealing with the lying spirit, it whispers in your ear. The seducing spirit lulls you into thinking and believing that there's no unlawful soul tie; everything is fine. Then comes the perverse spirit to follow up and twists your thoughts and emotions, and everything begins to crash in on you. Thankfully, the Holy Spirit will bring people across your path to tell truth and confront you.

But many just harden their hearts and carry a righteous indignation, which only strengthens the soul tie. They justify their actions, even make the Word fit into the box. A circle can fit easily into a square, but a square does not fit into a circle; it's four corners too large. We can make anything look like God, when in retrospect that's the deception. It is critical to know that if you are dealing and counseling someone, be careful. I always say men with men, and women with women. If possible, make that a mandate.

SATANIC RITUAL ABUSE (SRA)

Is satanic ritual abuse real? Yes. When people have surprise memories of what happened to them as a child, something triggered the past memory and their world comes crashing down. When someone tells me about this experience, I really listen to people, and ask the same question every time, "Holy Spirit, what has happened? Did this really happen?"

When you're trying to figure out what's going on in someone's life—or in your own situation— pray and fast, really seek the Father. That's what I do; and sometimes it's as if I go through time and space where God will take me back to a moment when the person was 3 years or 8 years of age, the time when something so traumatic happened that they still have it attached to them, like a thread that has to be cut. In that case, after the person is delivered, it's very important to make sure that—if you're binding up a lying, unclean spirit, and a spirit of infirmity—you fill that void with the Holy Spirit. I always pray for truth to prevail for healing, deliverance, or whatever needs to be filled. Something evil that has been taken out has to be replaced with good—the Holy Spirit.

When you were in darkness and then became saved, you came out of one place and stepped into another. I've heard many people say through the years that they wanted deliverance, and they went from place to place for help. But when I sit down and really start talking with them, it becomes obvious that they became used to and it liked the attention. When they went into a church, and the spirit manifested, all the attention was on them. Everyone gravitated to them—and then it was if Jesus wasn't even in the room. The saddest thing is to see people who say they want help, but they really don't because their identity for so long has been engraved in their thoughts—lies and deception from evil spirits. It takes time to deliver them from what keeps them bound up. Patience is important for you and for them.

> Satanic ritual abuse—sometimes known as ritual abuse, ritualistic abuse, organized abuse, sadistic ritual abuse, and other variants—was the subject of a moral panic (often referred to as the satanic panic) that originated in the United States in the 1980s, spreading throughout many parts of the world by the late 1990s. Allegations of SRA involved reports of physical and sexual abuse of people in the context of occult or satanic rituals. In its most extreme form, allegations involve a conspiracy of a worldwide SRA organization that includes the wealthy and powerful of the world elite in which children are abducted or bred for sacrifices, pornography and prostitution. (Source: Wikipedia)

Every day more of these cases come across my desk. My heart breaks for those caught up in the grip of satanism. Too many are going through horrific pain and can't get out or don't know how to. I pray that Jesus will appear to them and His presence will fill the rooms of despair and hopelessness. I break off all mind control right now that may be even be affecting this reader. Come, Your will be done, God. Send warrior angels, Lord, to guard and protect Your children, in Your name, Jesus, that is above every name.

WISDOM KEYS

When someone you are ministering to has gone through SRA, you must be very careful, for the person's psyche is fragile. The memories, for many, are very real. Many times, most who have gone through SRA have told me that one or both parents raised them in satanism. Make sure that when counseling and doing the deliverance your discernment is clear from the Father. I stress that point especially because of one story in particular. A young man told a story that drew people to his abusive childhood. In reality, he just wanted their attention. I saw people re-delivering this man, over and over. He told the story that he had been so mentally messed up, he couldn't work, was losing his apartment, had no food, etc. So, the church paid for all of his expenses, and it was all an act on his part. Even so, be aware that SRA is real, and many do suffer horribly, I always remind myself of that. Discerning spirits is critical always. In any situation, I always pray.

PRAYER

I pray and release Psalm 91:1-3:

> *Whoever dwells in the shelter of the Most High will rest in the shadow of the Almighty. I will say of the Lord, "He*

is my refuge and my fortress, my God, in whom I trust."
Surely he will save you from the fowler's snare and from
the deadly pestilence (NIV).

CONCLUSION

THE MOST IMPORTANT INSIGHT I CAN GIVE YOU IS TO PRAY AND follow after the Lord's heart—and to not give up! I have done numerous deliverances over the years, each being unique and different. Remember, not all deliverances will be the same; some will require additional attention or fasting or seeking. There are different levels of warfare.

Speaking personally to every stronghold I have discussed in this book, I want to say to each, "I hate you, I hate you, and I hate you even more!" It is my passion for justice and intolerance against the enemy's schemes that have allowed me through the years to see hundreds upon thousands of people healed, delivered, and set free with the Lord's help, which is not something I take lightly. He's allowed me to witness His love and salvation to countless numbers of witches and warlocks, to help expose the counterfeit and lies, to see the kingdom of darkness disarmed and dismantled.

When the Father calls you, He gives you the capacity and strength and energy you need to accomplish it. I can say that being

58 years of age today as I write this, the ministry I partner with the Father in is hardly ever difficult or really taxing. I have fought very hard to see freedom in my personal life, and I am very proud of who I am. It seems odd typing that, but it's true; I am. I have stayed the course and never compromised when it came to doing deliverance ministry, ever. I have never been driven by fame, money, or attention; not for anything. My only motivation has been to help those bound by darkness like I was, and help them know that there is true and lasting freedom available.

> *The Lord has opened his arsenal and brought out the weapons of his wrath, for the Sovereign Lord Almighty has work to do in the land of the Babylonians* (Jeremiah 50:25 NIV).

As an introduction, this book should serve to lay the foundation to prepare you for the next level, which I dive into with my *Demons and Angels* book and DVD series. All of my resources are intended to help you build a strong, solid foundation—to help you to recognize the enemy and how to discern and know what action steps need to be taken. Remember, you are the vessel, the vehicle on the road leading them to freedom! You are needed now more than ever. The foundation must be laid and be strong enough to withstand and handle the storms of life.

THE GREAT COMMISSION

> *Then the eleven disciples went away into Galilee, to the mountain which Jesus had appointed for them. When they saw Him, they worshiped Him; but some doubted.*
>
> *And Jesus came and spoke to them, saying, "All authority has been given to Me in heaven and on earth. Go therefore and make disciples of all the nations, baptizing them*

in the name of the Father and of the Son and of the Holy Spirit, teaching them to observe all things that I have commanded you; and lo, I am with you always, even to the end of the age." Amen (Matthew 28:16-20).

"...Not by might nor by power, but by My Spirit," says the Lord of hosts (Zechariah 4:6).

May the Lord train your hands for war, and your heart to follow His!

Till the end,
Angela

About Angela Greenig

Evangelist and revivalist Angela Greenig is a seasoned seer-warrior for Jesus Christ and a leading force in deliverance ministry. For more than thirty-five years she has been a defender of the faith and a voice for those who have no voice, traveling the world, preaching, and training the body of Christ. As founder of Angela Greenig Ministries International, a writer, and host of her own media channel, Angela has built and released deliverance and healing centers and ministries in many cities throughout the United States and nations of the world. Her teaching and insight come from years on the frontlines of spiritual warfare, fighting for the salvation and deliverance of people worldwide.

For more information, resources, and scheduling, please visit: www.angelagreenig.com.